A GRINGO'S GUIDE TO
AUTHENTIC
MEXICAN COOKING

WRITTEN BY
MAD COYOTE JOE

PHOTOGRAPHY BY
CHRISTOPHER MARCHETTI

NORTHLAND
PUBLISHING

This book is dedicated to the memory of my friend and teacher
Paul Elswick, whom I met standing at a border check station
twenty-one kilometers below the Mexican border at Nogales.

Special thanks to Kathy, without whose help this book would not have been possible.

I would also like to thank Scott Maish, Dave Jenney, and
Mike Threadgill; Don Mackey, Angela Discher, Anamaria Ceseña,
and our other friends at Jose Cuervo; and all the Vikings down at Joe's Grotto.

© 2001 by Joe Daigneault
Photographs © 2001 by Northland Publishing
All rights reserved.

This book may not be reproduced in whole or in part, by any means (with the exception of short quotes
for the purpose of review), without permission of the publisher. For information, address Permissions,
Northland Publishing, P. O. Box 1389, Flagstaff, Arizona 86002-1389.

The text type was set in Founder's Caslon 12
The display type was set in AG Old Face
Composed in the United States of America
Printed in China

Edited by Tammy Gales
Designed by Jennifer Schaber
Production supervised by Donna Boyd

All cooking temperatures in this book refer to the Fahrenheit scale.
The use of trade names does not imply an endorsement by the product manufacturer.

FIRST IMPRESSION 2001
ISBN 0-87358-787-1
04 05 06 07 08   8 7 6 5 4 3

Library of Congress Cataloging-in-Publication Data
Mad Coyote Joe, date
The gringo's guide to authentic Mexican cooking / by Mad Coyote Joe.
p. cm.
1. Cookery, Mexican. 2. Cookery, American--Southwestern style. I. Title.
TX716.M4 M34 2001
641.5972--dc21   2001044052

TABLE *of* CONTENTS

A NOTE *from the* AUTHOR

I hate to be the bearer of bad news, but when it comes to authentic Mexican food, you've most likely been deceived from the day you were born. The sadest part is that the ones who have been doing the deceiving are well-meaning people, the people you love and care about—everyone from Grandma to Mom and Dad, cooks and waiters, the nice lady in the drive-up window, and especially that cute little Spanish-speaking Chihuahua on TV!

If that isn't bad enough, the deceit usually comes in the form of a kindness. Maybe you're a little boy and your own mother pats you on the head and says, "Tonight we're having Mexican food!" After all, it's Mom, and if she says it's Mexican food, then by God it's Mexican food.

I tell you, every time you've been served canned refried beans, store-bought salsa, frozen guacamole, or drive-through tacos, burritos, tostadas, enchiladas, or fajitas piled high with yellow cheese and sour cream, you've been the victim of a national conspiracy. Well, someone has to stop the madness, and I mean now!

In the following pages you will experience authentic Mexican cooking first-hand, leaving behind the tourista vision of piñatas and straw sombreros to feel the relaxed pace of everyday life in the little villages and pueblos of Mexico. If you're one of those people who think cooking real Mexican food is difficult or complex because the ingredients are foreign, well, think again. Authentic Mexican cooking is simple if you know a few easy tricks. In no time at all, you too will be making authentic mole, fish tacos, tamales, calabacitas, mouth-watering enchiladas, and a dozen or so of the best salsas you've ever eaten. So enjoy these recipes with family and friends and say goodbye to gringo-style Mexican cooking forever!

MAD COYOTE JOE

LA COCINA MEXICANA

THE MEXICAN KITCHEN

If you're going to cross the line into authentic Mexican Cooking, you will need to know a few things about how the Mexican kitchen varies from the kitchens in Gringoland, U.S.A.

TOOLS OF THE MEXICAN KITCHEN

1. TORTILLA PRESS

The first time I made corn tortillas, I didn't. What I made was a big mess. The trick is using the right masa. I use a brand called "Maseca"—it's fantastic.

You need to cut two circles out of plastic (I use a zip-top bag) to keep the masa from sticking to the press. It takes a little time but once you've got it, they are so delicious and so much fun—not to mention your friends won't believe their eyes.

2. COMAL

The comal, which is like a round griddle, is essential for cooking corn tortillas. A good substitute is a crepe pan.

3. LIME PRESS

Forget tricks like rolling a lime before squeezing it or poking it with a fork. In Mexico, they go through millions of limes every day, so do what they do and use this handy tool.

4. MOLCAJETE

This is the centuries-old food processor. Salsa made in a molcajete is far superior to that made in an electric food processor, because it can grind spices and tear (not purée) tomatillos. See my recipe for Guadalajaran Salsa en Molcajete (page 54).

5. MOLINILLO

This is a wooden whisk for chocolate. The way to use this tool is to place the handle between the palms of your hands and rub them back and forth, working air into the chocolate and creating a froth.

INGREDIENTS OF THE MEXICAN TABLE

You may not have heard of some of these ingredients, but rest assured, they can be found in your local supermarket or specialty food store.

KEY LIMES

Here in the U.S. we use a Persian lime, which is larger, shinier, and greener than a key lime, and the flavor is more acidic and abrupt. The little Mexican or Key lime is more delicate in flavor and easier on your stomach.

CORN OIL

Oils are a great place to set the tone of a meal: for Italian meals, use olive oil; for Asian, use sesame oil mixed with a neutral oil like canola. Likewise, corn oil has a great flavor that goes well with Mexican cooking.

POSOLE

These corn kernels are treated with lime to remove the hard outer skin. It can be ground into masa harina to make tortillas and tamales, or served whole in soups like menudo and posole.

CHOCOLATE

Different from other chocolates, Mexican Chocolate is full of granulated sugar and contains a little canela. It is readily available in the U.S. Try my recipe for Mexican Hot Chocolate on page 132.

CILANTRO

I always tell people that with cilantro, the aromatic leaves of the coriander plant, the flavor is in the stems and the color is in the leaves. So when chopping cilantro, don't go to all the trouble of separating the leaves from the stems. Rinse it well and chop it fine. A few whole leaves make a beautiful garnish.

PILONCILLO

These raw Mexican sugar cones have an earthier flavor than their refined cousins, brown and granulated sugar.

EPAZOTE

When fresh, this stuff has a diesel smell. It is known as "Stink Weed" and is used for two reasons. Epazote has a primitive, herbaceous flavor that works well with many authentic Mexican dishes, and it stops the gas caused by many foods (organic Beano).

CUITLACOCHE

This one is miles away from the Gringo kitchen. It took me several years of knowing about it before I tried it—don't make the same mistake. The flavor is somewhat like a delicate, earthy truffle. Now prized as a specialty food, it is readily available in Latino markets, canned. Fresh cuitlacoche is a special-order item here in the U.S. Try sautéing it like a good mushroom with shallots and garlic. Yumm.

CANELA

Many cooks will tell you that canela is Mexican cinnamon, but this is not true. It's actually Cinnamomum Zeylanicum, or Ceylon Cinnamon from Sri Lanka. It's lighter in color and the flavor is very delicate compared with the cinnamon used in the United States.

TAMARINDO

The U.S. falls short when it comes to the chocolaty-brown pods of the tamarind tree. It seems every country on the planet (that has sunshine) uses tamarindo in one form or another, such as tamarind paste, syrup, pulp, and purée. It is also sold in bricks and made into a candy. The flavor is between dried apricot and key lime: tart-sweet and just plain wonderful. To see what it tastes like, try my recipe for the Tamarind Cooler, a refreshing drink from Mexico (page 131).

NOPALES

These young, tender Opuntia cactus pads are used in Nopales salad, which is often eaten in Mexico to ward off hunger when dinner is going to be a while. This works for a few reasons. Nopales are delicious and refreshing, with a flavor in between okra and green beans, and they are full of chromium, which regulates blood sugar. Many diabetics in Mexico eat nopales every day as a type of folk medicine.

CARBÓN

This mesquite charcoal is a necessity for Carne Asada (page 75). Pure Mesquite charcoal burns at about 1600 degrees. Charcoal briquettes burn at around 600 degrees, which is not hot enough to sear in the flavor of a good steak. Cooking with mesquite wood can cause an overpowering smoke flavor that can ruin a good meal.

FLOR DE JAMAICA

These dried flowers of the Hibiscus Sabdariffa make one of the most refreshing drinks I have ever had (Hibiscus Flower Tea, page 131).

QUESOS

Mexican cheeses are totally different from North American cheeses. Using the correct Mexican cheese really makes a meal. They are readily available in Latino markets. Here are a few names to look for:

OAXACA
A melting cheese

RANCHERO
Crumbly, great on tacos

COTIJA
Also crumbly, a little more pungent

PANELA
Soft, great with fresh fruit

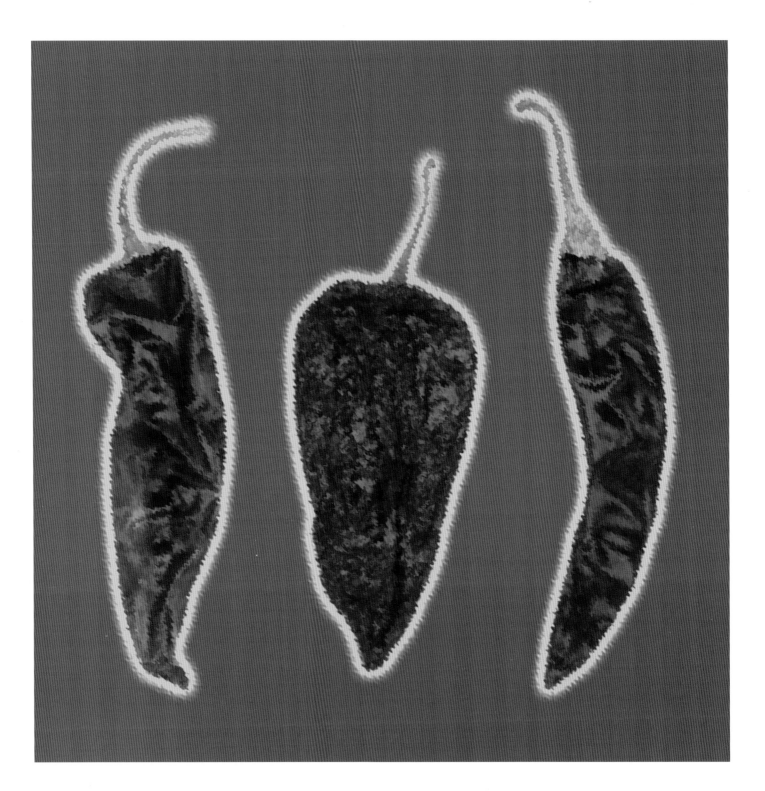

Ask any gringo about Mexican food and he'll say, "Well, they use a lot of jalapeños and green chiles." This is true, but it's only a little part of the whole story.

CHILES

CHILES

Chiles, which are the fruit of several different Capsicums (a genus of the nightshade family), seem to dominate the culinary landscape these days, especially in the form of Mexican food. If you want to know about authentic Mexican cooking, learn about dried chiles, the heart and soul of many Mexican dishes. The ancho is, without a doubt, the most popular chile in all of Mexico. It is used in moles and salsas, cut into strips as a garnish, or ground into a seasoning as chile powder. So that you know a little more about what you're doing in the kitchen—and can impress your friends, let's take a brief look at the history, selection, and use of chiles, as well as a closer look at some of the more popular varieties.

chile tepinas

A BRIEF HISTORY OF CHILES

October 12, 1492, 2:00 a.m., Rodrigo de Triana, a seaman sailing under Christopher Columbus on the Pinta, sights land in the new world. A quick "Land ho," and the culinary world is changed forever (not to mention the culture of the American natives).

Columbus is looking for, among other things, spices, and believes the small chiles growing wild in the new land to be a variety of black pepper. At that time, black pepper was the most expensive spice in the world and the Queen of Spain had it, right next to silver and gold, at the top of her laundry list of things Columbus was supposed to bring back home. Chiles, which are of no relation to black pepper at all, have been mistakenly called peppers ever since.

A native of the new world dating back as far as 8000 B.C., chiles were cultivated by the nomadic people of Central and South America as long ago as 7500 B.C.. By 900 to 1000 A.D., chiles were a major part of everyday life in the Incan empire. Varieties like the "rocoto" and "aji" were major crops and were also worshipped as a part of the Incan story of creation. Prior to Columbus, there were no chiles on the Asian, African, or European continents, and the Spanish quickly imported seeds for worldwide exportation.

SELECTING CHILES

When selecting chiles, look for those that have a deep, rich color. They should be clean, uniform in size, and free of blemishes or spots. Dried chiles should be a little pliable—the more brittle the dried chile, the older it is. The problem here is that over time, the essential oils that give the dried chiles their rich flavor evaporate. Dried chiles can be stored in a cool, dry place for up to six months.

MAKING SAUCES FROM CHILES

Toasting chiles will bring out their full color, flavor, and aroma. Always toast dried chiles before grinding them into a powder to give them more depth of flavor.

To make a basic sauce from dried chiles, toast them on a hot, dry comal or griddle until soft and pliable— about the texture of fruit leather. Remove chiles from comal and allow to cool. Remove stems, veins, and seeds. Place chiles and enough liquid (water or stock) to cover in a saucepan and simmer for 15 minutes. Pour in a blender, half a cup at a time, and purée. (Be careful—hot liquids expand in a blender and can spill out of the top and burn you.)

Pour the sauce through a wire sieve into a bowl, mashing it through with the back of a spoon until only the chile solids are left in the sieve. Discard chile solids. If sauce is too thin, return to heat and thicken. If you burn the chiles, even a little bit, discard and start over, as this will give the chiles and resulting sauce a bitter flavor (sort of the way I feel about most Mexican food in the United States).

ROASTING CHILES

Around my house, almost every time we light our barbecue, as soon as the coals are ready we roast 15 to 20 green chiles. They are delicious on the side of roasted meats, poultry, or fish and are an integral part of many Mexican dishes. They will keep in the refrigerator for 2 or 3 days and freeze well.

Roast the chiles over hot coals, turning often, until all the outside skin is blistered and dark brown. (You can also do this in the oven under the broiler.) If available, roast over mesquite charcoal, as this will impart a delicate smoky flavor. Put all the chiles into a plastic bag and twist the top closed. Let the chiles steam in their own heat for 10 minutes. The skin should peel off easily.

Remove seeds and stems. Chiles are often cross-bred and can vary in level of heat. The way I test for heat is to put one seed in my mouth. If it is extremely hot I will make sure that all seeds and veins are removed, as this is where most of the heat comes from. If it's still too hot, I reduce the amount of chile I use in the recipe.

THE HOLY TRINITY

In Mexico, many chiles have two or more names: one for the fresh form and one or more for various dried or smoked forms. The ancho is a good example of this. In its fresh form it is called a poblano.

The poblano is a dark green, heart-shaped chile about 5 inches long and about 3 inches wide at the shoulders. It is hotter than the Anaheim chile but milder than the jalapeño and is prized as the best chile for chiles rellenos. Here in the states, many grocers sell the poblano under the name "pasilla."

The pasilla ("little raisin"), also known as chile negro, is not a fresh chile at all, but instead, the dried form of the chilaca chile.

To further confuse things, not all dried poblanos are anchos; some, called mulato ("dark skinned"), are a distinctly different dried chile. Although similar in appearance to anchos, when held up to the light they appear much darker. Anchos can range from a deep, brownish-cherry red with slight orangish tints to dark mahogany in color, and they render more chile pulp than any other dried chile. They are much sweeter than other dried chiles and have a rich, earthy flavor that is a combination of mild fruits such as raisins or plums with hints of coffee or even tobacco. All this is wrapped in a deep, full-bodied, dark chile flavor with a mild to medium heat.

The ancho, like the mulato, is sold in three levels of quality, the most common being the ancho itself, which is the basic dried poblano. The second level, the mediano, is a little larger and has a thicker flesh. And the top grade, known as the primero, is seldom seen outside of Mexico. It is the largest, has the thickest flesh, is a near-perfect heart shape, and has no holes or blemishes.

The ancho, the mulato, and the pasilla are known in Mexico as the "Holy Trinity" of chiles, the basis for many moles. Finally, to confuse things even further, depending on the region, anchos are also known as chinos, chiles de guisar, chiles colorados, and, once again, chile de pasilla.

Let's take a look at some other chiles that you may want to get acquainted with.

dried chile ancho

FRESH CHILES

FROM MILD TO WILD

1. CHILACA

The chilaca is a deep, dark blackish green with hints of purple and brown. It's sort of a happy chocolate color. Curving and twisting, this chile is about 8 to 9 inches in length and approximately 1 inch across, and is seldom seen in the U.S. except in gardens. It is used in sauces or pickled, but is most commonly dried, going by the name pasilla ("little raisin") or chile negro.

MODERATE

GRINGO **APPROVED** **Heat: 3–4**

2. MANZANO

I love to use this chile as a garnish because of the beautiful contrast between its black seeds and bright yellow to orange flesh. The name means apple-like. It has a distinctly rich, very hot, fruity flavor. The flesh is soft but the skin is a little tough. It measures about 3 inches tall and 2½ inches wide, and its shape is halfway between a poblano and a bell pepper. It works well in rajas, rellenos, and salsas and is also known as chile caballo, chile rocoto, or chile perón.

DANGER

GRINGO **KILLER** **Heat: 7–8**

3. HABANERO

This is the hottest chile in the world. The name means "from Havana." Colors include any combination of yellow, orange, red, and green. In this part of the world, habaneros grow to roughly the size of a ping-pong ball, but in the Yucatan are known to grow as large as a medium-sized bell pepper. Once you get past the heat, this delicious little wonder has a rich, sweet, earthy flavor that is unmistakable. They're great roasted or in salsas, and I use them to help add a Caribbean flavor to dishes and sauces.

DANGER

GRINGO **KILLER** **Heat: 10**

4. JALAPEÑO

This is the most popular fresh chile in the U.S. Dark green, bullet-shaped, and about 2 to 3 inches long, it packs a good medium heat. Great in salsas, chile verde, or any place you want heat. The darker the hotter, and the black ones—watch out!

GRINGO BEWARE

Heat: 5–6

5. THAI

When ripe, this chile is around 3½ to 4 inches long and ¼ inch wide, and the colors run from red and orange to deep green. I use this chile whenever I want to add heat to Asian cooking. It has a distinct, earthy chile flavor that is very hot and goes well with meat, poultry, and fish.

GRINGO KILLER

Heat: 7–8

6. GÜERO

The name refers to pale or white skin. (The many folks down in Mexico that are fair-complected and of European descent are affectionately called güeros.) This chile is about the same size as a jalapeño but has a pointed tip. North of the border it is known as a "Yellow Hot." Used in moles and salsas, it has an intense, fiery flavor. I use it for adding heat more than flavor. Güero also refers to any pale-skinned chile such as the Hungarian wax or banana pepper.

GRINGO BEWARE

Heat: 5–7

7. SERRANO

This chile has a distinct flavor and is great in salsas, on sandwiches, or eaten raw. It is bullet-shaped, 2 to 3 inches long, half an inch across, and hotter than the jalapeño.

GRINGO BEWARE

Heat: 6–7

8. FRESNO

Often mistaken for a red jalapeño, the Fresno is similar in shape but its point is narrower; it's 2 to 2½ inches long and ¾ of an inch across. Its flavor is rich and sweet, and it makes a good substitute for jalapeños when you want a bright red color. It is outstanding raw, in salsas, or in marinades.

GRINGO APPROVED

Heat: 6–7

9. POBLANO

Dark green and heart-shaped, this chile is 5 to 6 inches long, has a medium heat, and is my favorite for rellanos. This delicious chile embodies all that is good about chiles. It adds a great medium heat and rich flavor when used fresh, or roast this chile and it is the perfect side dish for anything you want to give that full-bodied chile flavor to.

GRINGO APPROVED

Heat: 5–6

10. ANAHEIM

This is the most common mild green chile available in the United States, and it is often found in a can. The Anaheim is light green in color and 5 to 6 inches long. It is usually mild, but be careful—sometimes it's very hot. It is often used for roasting or in chiles rellenos.

GRINGO FRIENDLY

Heat: 2–3

ROCOTILLO *(Not pictured.)*

Known as "Gringo Killers" in South America, these little devils are a great addition to salsa or seviche. They are also served roasted or pickled. The rocotillo is a squatty little member of the habanero family and has a similar flavor: fruity, full-bodied, and very hot. It measures about 1 inch tall and 1½ inches across.

GRINGO KILLER

Heat: 7–9

NEW MEXICO *(Not pictured.)*

This chile, legendary in the southwestern United States, is often sold as a Hatch green chile. Although similar to the Anaheim in shape and size, it has a greater depth of green chile flavor. It is one of the best chiles for roasting and making chile verde. I love to serve them roasted and peeled on the side of a Mesquite-grilled ribeye steak.

GRINGO FRIENDLY

Heat: 2–3

SCOTCH BONNET *(Not pictured.)*

Related to the habanero and very similar in shape, but smaller, this chile is about 1½ inches across and the same up and down. Usually yellow to light orange, it also runs green to red. The Scotch Bonnet is the ingredient that gives Jamaican jerk its fire. It is known as Levanta los Muertos, which roughly translates to "raise the dead." This chile is basically the habanero of the Caribbean Islands.

GRINGO KILLER

Heat: 9–10

DRIED CHILES

RATTLESNAKES AND RAISINS

CASCABEL *(Not pictured.)*

The cascabel, meaning "rattle," makes a sound like a baby's rattle when shaken, and the word is also a nickname for the rattlesnake. It has a deep, full-bodied, lightly smoky flavor and is used in sauces, soups, and stews. It's also a nice addition to chile powder. It measures 1 inch in length and ¼ inch across, and are a dirty mahogany in color.

MODERATE / GRINGO APPROVED **Heat: 3–4**

1. CHIPOTLE

This is a large, dried, peat-smoked jalapeño. Leathery in appearance with a chocolatey, dull tan color, it measures 2 to 3 inches long and about 1 inch across. Its unmistakable mildly sweet, hot, smoky flavor is a must for Mexican cooking. Approximately 20 percent of all jalapeños grown in Mexico become chipotles. This little gem will take your salsas and sauces to a new level. Commonly available canned in adobo sauce in the U.S., they really spice up homemade barbecue sauce.

 HOT! / GRINGO BEWARE **Heat: 6–7**

2. DE ARBOL

The name means "chile from a tree" or "treelike." You've most likely seen this very hot chile in Asian cooking, especially in Thai food. It has a blood-red color and measures 3 to 4 inches in length and ¼ inch across. Try toasting these chiles and adding them to your favorite salsa.

DANGER / GRINGO KILLER **Heat: 7–8**

3. GUAJILLO

This is my favorite chile for roast pork due to its rich, sweet flavor. Similar in appearance to the New Mexico red chile, it has a milder red chile flavor and measures 5 to 6 inches long and 1½ to 2 inches across. It is great in chile powders, moles, enchilada sauces, and salsas.

MODERATE / GRINGO APPROVED **Heat: 3**

MORA *(Not pictured.)*

This is a small dried, smoked, red jalapeño similar to the chipotle but usually smaller. Deep brownish-red with a little shine on the skin, it has a sweeter fruity flavor but is still very hot. It measures 1 to 1½ inches in length and ½ to ¾ of an inch across.

 HOT! / GRINGO BEWARE **Heat: 6–7**

4. NEGRO/PASILLA

The dried form of the chilaca chile, pasilla roughly means "little raisin," and looking at the almost black, wrinkly skin, one can see why. With an abrupt, even curt and yet mildly sweet flavor, it measures up to 7 inches long and 1½ to 2 inches across. One of the three chiles (ancho, mulato, and pasilla) that make up what is known as the "Holy Trinity" of chiles, it is essential in making classic mole. When ground to a bright red powder, it is outstanding in seafood dishes.

MODERATE
GRINGO APPROVED

Heat: 3–5

6. PIQUÍN

DANGER
GRINGO KILLER

Related to the chile tepín, this chile is very hot and has a slightly sweet, earthy, and yet smoky flavor. It measures ½ inch long and ¼ inch across.

Heat: 8–9

5. NEW MEXICO

This is the most common dried chile in the U.S., often used in ristras (you know, those strings of dried chiles you always see hanging from the porch of adobe buildings on post cards from New Mexico). It is essential in making good old American red chili and chile powder. It measures 5 to 6 inches long and 1½ to 2 inches across, and it is also known as the colorado chile. It is one of my favorite chiles for enchilada sauce.

MODERATE
GRINGO APPROVED

Heat: 3–4

7. PULLA

This is a wonderful chile that I toast and use in my favorite salsa, Guadalajaran Salsa en Molcajete (recipe page 54). The flavor is halfway between a guajillo chile and a chile de arbol. Use it anywhere you want medium heat and a deep, full-bodied, red chile flavor. Its color is blood red, and it's shaped like a fat chile de arbol, measuring 5 inches long and ½ to ¾ of an inch across.

HOT!
GRINGO BEWARE

Heat: 5–6

8. TEPÍN

I love these little fireballs. Harvested in the wild, these chiles are served on the side with soup or tacos or used to add heat wherever you may need it. They are round and measure about ¼ inch across. It is speculated that these, or a similar variety, are what Columbus mistook for a relation of black pepper.

DANGER
GRINGO KILLER

Heat: 8–10

DESAYUNO

The average breakfast in the United States often goes something like this: You get up, walk half-asleep into the kitchen, press the button on the coffee maker, and go take a quick shower. Then it's back to the kitchen to make those little toaster breakfast pastries; "Mmmm, I think I'll have the Queso Mexicali." Then you kiss your dog, pat the kids on the head, and run to the car with a cup of coffee in one hand and that delicious prefabricated stale breakfast thing in the other.

MEXICANO

That is, of course, when you have the extra time to make breakfast. On the days you don't, it's good old "Eggs McDrive-Thru." Both breakfasts seem to get choked down while fighting traffic and planning your day. The average household in Mexico, while it doesn't have five hundred channels on the tube, does have the time to sit down and eat a decent breakfast at a relaxed pace before taking on the burdens of the workday.

In this chapter, you'll discover new ways to use corn tortillas and dried chiles with some traditional Mexican favorites you may not have tried—but will absolutely love—like chilaquiles and migas. In no time at all you'll be making huevos rancheros, posole, and menudo just like they serve in good Mexican-food restaurants every Sunday morning here in the States.

Then, after you've made your first authentic Mexican breakfast, I want you to do one more thing. Relax, slow down, talk a little with your spouse and kids while enjoying your own cooking, and have a slow, second cup of coffee. As they say in Mexico, "The work will still be there."

HUEVOS CON MACHACA

EGGS WITH DRIED BEEF

I live forty miles outside of town, and I try not to drive in too often. However, when I do have to go in for anything, I make sure to hurry and get to my favorite little restaurant before 11:00 a.m. when they stop serving Huevos con Machaca—my all-time favorite Mexican breakfast.

½ cup dried machaca (recipe page 74)

1 teaspoon corn oil

2 teaspoons minced white onion

½ plum tomato, finely chopped

1 serrano chile, seeded and finely chopped

2 eggs

Salt to taste

Soak the machaca in a little bowl of cold water for 1 minute. Drain and then squeeze out all excess moisture. Tear the meat into shreds.

Sauté the onion in the oil until translucent. Add the meat, tomato, and chile, and sauté until tomato is cooked but do not brown the meat. Stir in the eggs and mix well. Cook until eggs are set. Taste and adjust salt. Serve immediately with refried beans and tortillas.

MAKES 1 SERVING

CHILAQUILES COLORADOS

CHILAQUILES WITH RED SAUCE

At the finer hotels in Guadalajara, breakfast is served buffet-style. The fare is usually traditional Mexican, including fresh fruit, fresh salsas, carne asada, refried beans, handmade tortillas and, of course, chilaquiles (see photo page 19).

SAUCE

8 dried guajillo chiles

2 cups consomé de pollo (recipe page 45)
or chicken broth

1 clove garlic, minced

¼ teaspoon Mexican oregano

½ teaspoon ground cumin

Corn oil for frying tortillas

10 corn tortillas, cut into wedges

¼ white onion, julienned

3 tablespoons queso Cotija

GRINGO
FRIENDLY

Toast the chiles on a hot, dry comal until soft and pliable. Remove chiles from comal and allow to cool down a little. Remove stems and seeds. Place the chiles and all remaining sauce ingredients in a saucepan and simmer for 15 minutes. Pour into a blender, ¾ of a cup at a time, and purée. (Be careful—hot liquids expand in a blender and can spill out of the top and burn you). Pour the sauce through a sieve into a bowl, mashing with the back of a spoon until only chile solids are left. Discard chile solids and set sauce aside.

In a large, heavy frying pan, heat about an inch of corn oil over medium heat until hot enough that a piece of tortilla dropped in oil immediately floats to the top and bubbles. Fry the tortilla wedges, a handful at a time, until just crisp. Remove them from the oil and drain on paper towels; salt immediately.

Preheat oven to 350 degrees. Pour half of the sauce into a baking dish, arrange the tortilla wedges flat in the bottom of the dish, and pour in remaining sauce. Bake for 10 minutes. Garnish with white onion and crumbled queso Cotija.

SERVES 4 TO 6

HUEVOS RANCHEROS

RANCH-STYLE EGGS

This is the only way to start a Saturday morning, unless you make a good menudo. By not deep-frying the tortillas you will greatly reduce the fat and lighten the taste.

2 (5-inch) corn tortillas

A little butter for frying eggs

2 extra-large eggs

¼ cup Salsa de Tomatillo Verde, warm (recipe page 64)

1 tablespoon crumbled queso Ranchero

GARNISH

Chopped lettuce

Chopped tomato

Avocado slices

In a hot, dry comal or frying pan, lightly fry the tortillas until soft and pliable. Put the tortillas in a tortilla warmer or on a plate and cover with a clean dish towel.

Put the tortillas on a dinner plate and place one egg, fried to your liking in a little butter, on each tortilla. Spoon 2 tablespoons warm Salsa de Tomatillo Verde over each egg and top with crumbled cheese. Garnish and serve with Mexican rice on the side.

MAKES 1 SERVING

OPPOSITE: *(clockwise from bottom) Huevos Rancheros (recipe above) with Salsa Ranchera (recipe page 67), Chilaquiles Colorados (recipe page 17), and Huevos a la Mexicana (recipe page 21).*

HUEVOS REVUELTOS CON CHORIZO

SCRAMBLED EGGS WITH CHORIZO

At good Mexican restaraunts on Sunday mornings, you will see either Menudo, Posole, or Chorizo with eggs. This breakfast is best served with fresh tortillas and a little hot coffee. It is an age-old Mexican treat.

Corn oil for frying chorizo

4 ounces chorizo

4 eggs

MODERATE

GRINGO APPROVED

Slowly fry the chorizo in a lightly oiled pan until fully cooked. Drain the pan of excess grease. Add the eggs and stir together. Cook until eggs are set. Serve immediately.

SERVES 2

MIGAS

Down in Mexico, nothing goes to waste. This is a delicious way to use up day-old tortillas. It makes a wonderful breakfast, and it's my wife's favorite.

4 tablespoons corn oil

4 corn tortillas, cut into thin strips

Salt to taste

½ cup chopped, plum tomato

¼ cup chopped, white onion

2 serrano chiles, seeded and chopped

4 eggs

MODERATE

GRINGO APPROVED

Heat 3 ½ tablespoons of the corn oil over medium-high heat until very hot. Fry the tortilla strips until they start to crisp. Remove from oil, salt, and drain on paper towels. Heat remaining oil in a clean skillet and stir-fry the chopped tomato, onion, and chiles for 30 seconds. Add tortilla strips.

Beat the eggs with a pinch of salt. Pour eggs over the vegetables in the skillet and cook, stirring often, until fully cooked. Serve with salsa and homemade refried beans or rice.

SERVES 4

HUEVOS A LA MEXICANA

MEXICAN STYLE EGGS

This is good home cooking down in Mexico. Try serving it with fresh, hot corn tortillas and guacamole. To make Huevos con Nopales, add 1 cup cooked nopales to the sauté. Nopales are a delicious vegetable—it's just a little hard for the average gringo to get over the fact that he's eating a cactus.

1 tablespoon corn oil

1 tablespoon bacon drippings

1 jalapeño chile, minced

½ white onion, finely chopped

1 Roma tomato, finely chopped

8 eggs

1 teaspoon salt

In a frying pan, sauté the jalapeño, onion, and tomato in the oil and bacon drippings until soft but not browned. Beat the eggs and salt together and add to the frying pan; cook to desired consistency.

SERVES 4

PAPAS CON CHORIZO

POTATOES WITH SPICY PORK SAUSAGE

This dish is so good for breakfast when served in warm tortillas with Salsa de Tomatillo Verde (page 64), and chopped cilantro and white onion on the side. It also makes a great filling for tacos using about ¼ cup for each one (makes 12 tacos).

1 pound new potatoes, halved

2 teaspoons corn oil

½ pound chorizo, not in casings

½ white onion, finely chopped

Boil the potatoes for 12 to 15 minutes or until fork-tender. Remove from water and peel; set aside. Fry the chorizo in the corn oil for 10 minutes, breaking it up as you cook. Remove chorizo from pan; set aside. Drain excess grease from pan, leaving enough to coat the bottom of the pan. Fry the onion and potato until browned, stirring often to avoid burning.

Add the chorizo and fry for a few minutes more to warm chorizo. Stir well and serve.

SERVES 4

POSOLE

In Sonora, Mexico, posole is made in big, square, five-gallon metal cans like the ones they used to sell salad oil in twenty years ago. They bury the can in the ground, build a fire over it, and cook it for a day. It's a big hit at breakfast and for fiestas. As this is a gringo's guide, I've reworked the recipe for your kitchen. This is one of my most-requested recipes.

2 pounds roasted pork or any cooked poultry

3 (14½-ounce) cans white hominy, drained

1 teaspoon whole Mexican oregano

3 cloves fresh garlic, minced

1 teaspoon ground cumin

⅓ cup New Mexico mild red chile powder

2 (48-ounce) cans chicken broth

GARNISH

2 cups finely chopped purple cabbage

1 white onion, finely chopped

1 bunch red radishes, washed and thinly sliced

1 bunch fresh cilantro, washed and diced

2 teaspoons chile tepín or cayenne pepper

2 fresh key limes, cut into wedges

GRINGO
FRIENDLY

Place pork, hominy, oregano, garlic, cumin, New Mexico mild chile powder, and chicken broth in a large slow-cooker. Heat on medium for 5 to 6 hours or longer. Stir occasionally. Serve in large soup bowls topped with a little of each of the following: purple cabbage, white onion, radish slices, and cilantro. Crush 1 chile tepín into each bowl or add a pinch of cayenne pepper and a squeeze of fresh lime.

SERVES 8

MENUDO

Menudo is a favorite for a weekend Mexican breakfast. It's a sure cure for a hangover. It's so popular that in many parts of Mexico, there are parlors for menudo where people can go on Saturday night after drinking and dancing. If you really want to get past being a gringo, you've got to try menudo!

3 pounds tripe, well washed

2 white onions, chopped

Water

3 cloves garlic, minced

1 tablespoon salt

1 teaspoon whole Mexican oregano

1 (28-ounce) can white hominy

GARNISH

1 bunch cilantro, cleaned and finely chopped

1 white onion, chopped

2 fresh limes, cut into wedges

In a large stock pot place the tripe, onions, garlic, salt, oregano and water to cover by 2 inches; bring to a boil. Simmer on low all day (at least 6 hours). Add a little water now and then as needed.

When the tripe is tender remove it from the pot and cut into ½-inch cubes. Return it to the pot, add hominy, and cook for 1 hour more. Serve in large soup bowls with a little cilantro, a little onion, and a lime wedge on the side.

SERVES 6 TO 8

23

FRIJOLES, ARROZ,

A while back, while driving in downtown Phoenix, I saw a little out-of-the-way place with a sign that read, "Authentic Mexican Food." I was hungry (what's new?), so I went in. I asked the waitress, "Do you make your beans from scratch?"

y VERDURAS

"Of course we do," she said. "You see, we have a chef that comes in every morning and blah, blah, blah…" She went on for five minutes. From this lengthy explanation I should have known something was wrong, but I ordered anyway. I knew I was in trouble when I saw my plate coming piled high with sour cream, chopped tomatoes, and iceberg lettuce. After closer examination, I discovered ring marks still visible in my refried beans; obviously the "chef" had spooned them directly out of a can. To top it off, they were covered with melted cheddar cheese. I got up, paid, and left hungry.

If your Mexican food experiences include canned refried beans, those quick rice mixes, or the same old tired vegetables, this chapter will change the way you look at these simple side dishes forever. The beans, rice, and vegetables of Mexico are so much more than something to serve with tacos or enchiladas; they are the backbone of a great authentic Mexican meal. They sort of tie the whole plate together. They also make a fantastic meal just by themselves. And, as with so many dishes from Mexico, there are literally hundreds of recipes. So here are some of my favorites. Trust me, they'll soon be your favorites, too!

CUITLACOCHE

CORN FUNGUS

Okay, this one may sound a little weird. Cuitlacoche's closest translation is "corn fungus." Before you make up your mind, remember that all mushrooms are fungus, and that's how I think about this wonderful, earthy-tasting dish. You'll love it.

¼ cup corn oil

2 green onions, finely chopped

2 cloves garlic, chopped

4 cups chopped zucchini

1 cup corn

2 cups canned Cuitlacoche or 4 cups fresh if you can find it

3 serrano chiles, chopped

½ teaspoon salt

1½ tablespoons chopped epazote or cilantro

MODERATE

GRINGO APPROVED

Fry the green onions and garlic until soft but not browned. Add the zucchini and fry until excess moisture is almost gone. Add all other ingredients except epazote or cilantro and cook until tender. Add the epazote and saute a few minutes more. Remove from heat and allow to stand for 10 minutes, covered, to let flavors blend. Serve warm.

SERVES 6

FRIJOLES DE OLLA

BEANS IN A POT

Traditionally, olla (OY-ya) refers to a clay or earthenware pot, as in Café de Olla (coffee made in a clay pot, recipe page 132) but you can also use any big, heavy pot you may have. The fun thing about using an olla is taking it to the table for serving and using individual earthenware bowls.

1 pound pink or pinto beans

1 tablespoon white vinegar

½ white onion, finely chopped

2 tablespoons lard or corn oil

1 manzano chile, seeded and finely chopped

(if unavailable, habanero is a good substitute)

Pinch of Mexican oregano

Salt to taste

Sort through the beans and remove any foreign material. Rinse very well. Place in a large bowl, add vinegar, and cover with water. Let stand overnight.

Drain water and rinse well. Place beans in olla or big pot and pour in 12 cups water. Add all other ingredients except the salt. Bring to a rolling boil for 10 minutes and then reduce heat to medium low and simmer for about 3 hours or until beans are tender. Add salt and continue simmering for 30 minutes more. Serve with warm corn tortillas and queso Oaxaca.

SERVES 8

FRIJOLES REFRITOS

REFRIED BEANS

Have you noticed that the refried beans in a real Mexican food restaurant are totally different from canned refried beans? They're just so creamy and rich. Brace yourself—the reason for this wonderful flavor might frighten you… It's… lard. There, I've said it. The very word "lard" is enough to cause the average gringo to flee.

My personal problem with lard is not so much the fat as the flavor. Commercially processed lard is missing the roast pork flavor that "home rendered" lard has. Therefore, it only adds fat, and animal fat at that. A good substitute for lard is an equal amount mixture of 2 parts corn oil and 1 part bacon drippings.

This is a basic recipe for Mexican beans. They are stored, and only what is to be eaten is reheated or "refried." In different parts of Mexico regional flavors are added—everything from cream, beer, and rum to tomatoes, onions, and jalapeños.

And remember, if the beans get a little dry when you're refrying them, you can always do what they do down in Mexico—Just add a little more lard!

2 cups dry pink or pinto beans

1 cup lard

At least 5 cups water, room temperature

Salt to taste

Remove any foreign material from beans and rinse well. In a large, heavy pot, coat the beans well with ¼ cup of the lard. Add water. Bring to a boil for 5 minutes, reduce heat to medium-low and cover. Simmer for 2 hours. Check now and then to see if a little more water is needed, stirring each time you check. In the last 30 minutes of cooking, salt to taste.

In a separate heavy skillet, heat ½ cup of the lard. Using a slotted spoon, place about 1 cup of the beans in the heated lard. Mash with a wooden bean masher or fork. Add a little of the liquid from the pot of beans, stir, and repeat the process until all of the beans and liquid are incorporated.

SERVES 6 TO 8

FRIJOLES A LA CHARRA

CHARRO STYLE BEANS

The average gringo thinks refried beans are the only way beans are served in Mexico. This recipe is another typical Mexican recipe. You'll find these beans all over Mexico but especially around Mexico city.

3 cups (about 1 pound) dried pink beans
1 tablespoon white vinegar
6 cups water
1 bottle of Negra Modelo Mexican beer
¾ pound bacon, fried, crumbled, and
    drained (save 2 tablespoons
    of the drippings for finish)
1 white onion, finely chopped
2 cloves garlic, minced
1 tablespoon corn oil
4 poblano chiles, roasted, peeled,
    and chopped

2 dried chipotle chiles
2 teaspoons kosher salt
1 teaspoon ground cumin
1 teaspoon whole Mexican oregano
1½ tablespoons chopped epazote
    or cilantro

GARNISH
Fresh corn tortillas, chopped cilantro,
chiles tepinas, lime wedges,
finely chopped white onion

FINISHING INGREDIENTS
2 tablespoons bacon drippings
4 cloves garlic, minced
1 white onion, finely chopped
4 Roma tomatoes, chopped
1 jalapeño chile, finely chopped
½ teaspoon Mexican oregano
⅓ cup 100% pure agave tequila

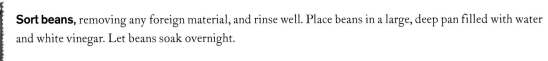

Sort beans, removing any foreign material, and rinse well. Place beans in a large, deep pan filled with water and white vinegar. Let beans soak overnight.

Remove beans from water and rinse well. Discard soaking water. Place beans, 6 cups fresh water, beer, bacon, onion, garlic, oil, chiles, salt, cumin, oregano, and cilantro or epazote in a large pot over medium-high heat and bring to a boil. Reduce heat and simmer for a few hours until beans are tender. Using a bean masher or fork, mash just a few of the beans, enough to slightly thicken the bean broth.

TO FINISH:

In a skillet over medium heat, sauté the onion and garlic in the saved bacon drippings for about 5 minutes or until lightly browned. Add all other finishing ingredients and simmer for about 5 minutes; add to pot of beans. Simmer for ½ hour more. Adjust seasoning. Serve with warm tortillas and other garnishes on the side.

SERVES 6 TO 8

29

ARROZ A LA MEXICANA

MEXICAN RICE

Rice is an integral part of the Mexican kitchen. It is used in main courses, drinks, and even desserts. This is a good basic recipe that adds the finishing touch to any Mexican main course.

1 ½ cups long-grain rice

1 cup diced jitomate or plum tomatoes

2 cloves garlic, minced

¼ white onion, chopped

¼ cup corn oil

2 (14 ½-ounce) cans chicken broth

⅓ cup frozen corn

⅓ cup diced carrots

⅓ cup frozen baby peas

1 small zucchini, diced

1 teaspoon mild red New Mexico chile powder

½ teaspoon kosher salt

Soak the rice in very hot water for 10 minutes. Drain the rice and rinse in cold water. Let all excess water drain off.

In a blender, process the tomatoes, garlic, and onion until smooth. Lightly brown the rice in the oil in a large frying pan over medium/medium-high heat. Stir often and do not let stick. Add tomato mixture and continue to cook for about 7 minutes; continue stirring. Stir in broth, vegetables, chile powder, and salt, and mix. As soon as the rice comes to a boil, turn heat to low and cover for 20 minutes. Stir before serving.

SERVES 6 TO 8

OPPOSITE: *(clockwise from bottom) Arroz a la Mexicana (recipe above), Arroz Verde a la Mexicana (recipe page 32), and Frijoles a la Charra (recipe page 29).*

ARROZ VERDE A LA MEXICANA

MEXICAN GREEN RICE

You'll find this simple, savory dish more often in homes in Mexico than in the restaurants there. It's almost unheard of in Mexican restaurants here in the United States. It goes especially well with poultry and seafood.

1 ½ cups long-grain rice

¾ cup loosely packed, chopped, flat-leaf parsley

¾ cup loosely packed, chopped epazote or cilantro

1 clove garlic, diced

2 cans (14½-ounce) chicken or vegetable broth

¼ cup corn oil

2 roasted poblano chiles

¼ cup chopped white onion

1 small zucchini, diced

1 cup corn

½ teaspoon salt

GARNISH

1 poblano chile, roasted, peeled, and sliced into strips

1 red bell pepper, roasted, peeled, and sliced into strips

MODERATE

GRINGO APPROVED

Soak the rice in a bowl of very hot water for 10 minutes. Drain the rice and rinse in cold water; let all excess water drain off.

In a blender, process the parsley, cilantro or epazote, garlic, and half of the broth until smooth.

Lightly brown the rice in the oil in a large, heavy frying pan over medium heat. When rice is golden brown, add the diced chiles and onion and continue cooking until onions are translucent. Stir often and do not let stick. Add broth mixture from blender and continue to cook for about 7 minutes, stirring often. Add zucchini, corn, remaining broth, and salt and stir well. As soon as the rice comes to a full boil, turn heat to low and cover for 20 minutes. Stir before serving. Garnish with strips of roasted chile.

SERVES 6 TO 8

ARROZ BLANCO

WHITE RICE

This is a basic example of the white rice served all over Mexico, but don't stop at serving it with Mexican food. Try this rice dish anywhere you would usually serve regular white rice.

1 ½ cups long-grain white rice

⅓ cup corn oil

¼ white onion, minced

1 clove garlic, minced

3½ cups consomé de pollo (recipe page 45) or chicken broth

¼ cup of any frozen or fresh vegetables such as corn, carrots, peas, or beans

Salt to taste

Soak the rice in very hot water for 10 minutes. Drain the rice and rinse in cold water. Let all excess water drain off.

Lightly brown the rice in the oil in a large frying pan over medium/medium-high heat. Stir often and do not let stick. Add onion and garlic. Cook until translucent, about 5 minutes; continue stirring. Stir in broth, vegetables, and salt. As soon as the rice comes to a boil, turn heat to low and cover for 20 minutes. Stir before serving.

SERVES 8

RAJAS CON LIMÓN

CHILE STRIPS WITH LIME

Rajas con Limón is a popular side dish served throughout Mexico. This recipe is quite hot. It can be made with any roasted chile.

4 large manzano chiles, roasted, seeds and
veins removed, and cut into ¼-inch strips
(if unavailable, habanero chiles are a good substitute)
¼ medium white onion, julienned
Juice of 6 key limes (about ⅓ of a cup)
Salt to taste
Pinch or two of Mexican oregano

GRINGO
KILLER

Mix all ingredients together in a glass bowl. Cover and refrigerate overnight. Keeps in the refrigerator for 5 or 6 days.

MAKES 1½ CUPS

ELOTE ASADO CON LIMÓN Y CHILE

GRILLED CORN WITH LIME AND CHILE

Elote Asado is very popular all over Mexico. You'll see it being served at roadside stands and at street fairs. Once you try this, you'll never look at an ear of corn the same way again!

8 ears of fresh corn, husks removed

½ stick butter

2 limes, quartered

Mild red chile powder to taste

Salt to taste

GRINGO
FRIENDLY

Boil corn until tender, about 6 minutes. Coat with butter. Grill over medium heat, allowing grill marks. Remove from heat; squeeze lime over corn and sprinkle with chile powder. Salt to taste.

SERVES 6 TO 8

CALABACITAS

SQUASH

This is a great summertime side dish. Melt in a handful of shredded queso Oaxaca after you've cooked this and your kids will go crazy.

2 tablespoons corn oil

¼ medium white onion, finely chopped

1 clove garlic, minced

1 medium tomato, finely chopped

1 jalapeño chile, finely chopped, or 1 poblano chile,
roasted and peeled

4 medium (about 1 pound) zucchini (or your favorite
summer squash), chopped into ½-inch cubes

Pinch of Mexican oregano

Salt to taste

MODERATE

GRINGO APPROVED

Fry the onion and garlic over medium heat until just translucent but not browned. Add the tomato and jalapeño and continue frying for about 5 more minutes. Add the zucchini, oregano, and salt. Cover and cook for 5 more minutes. Remove lid and continue frying, stirring constantly, until excess juice is absorbed.

SERVES 6

OPPOSITE: *(clockwise from bottom) Rajas con Lemón (recipe page 34), Calabacitas (recipe above), and Elote Asado con Lemón y Chile (recipe page 35).*

ENSALADA DE NOPAL

PRICKLY-PEAR SALAD

This recipe works well with store-bought, bottled nopales, but skip the boiling step and reduce the amount used here to three cups, as nopales shrink while cooking.

6 cups fresh, young nopales, cut into ½-inch squares

3 bunches green onion

6 tablespoons plus 1 teaspoon salt

1 fresh jalapeño chile, diced (do not remove seeds)

2 medium plum tomatoes, diced

¼ cup finely chopped white onion

½ bunch cilantro, chopped

Juice of 2 key limes

½ teaspoon Mexican oregano

In a medium stock pot, cover the nopales with at least 3 inches of water. Add 1 bunch of green onions and 2 tablespoons salt; bring to a rolling boil. Let boil for ten minutes. Remove from heat and pour into a colander. Discard green onion; rinse nopales in cold water until cool. Repeat the boiling with onion and salt and rinsing process three times. This will remove the viscous material (slimy stuff) from the cactus pads. The nopales will now be about half the amount you started with.

Mix nopales, jalapeño, tomato, white onion, cilantro, lime juice, oregano, and remaining teaspoon salt. Let stand for 45 minutes for flavors to blend. Serve at room temperature.

SERVES 6 TO 8

CHIPOTLES EN ESCABECHE

PICKLED CHIPOTLE CHILES

With their hot, smoky flavor, pickled chipotle chiles are a common side dish served with grill roasted meats, fish, and poultry.

⅓ pound dried chipotle chiles, quickly rinsed and paper-towel dried

½ cup corn oil

3 medium white onions, chopped

4 cloves garlic, minced

3 cups white vinegar

2¼ cups water

5 sprigs fresh marjoram

6 sprigs fresh thyme

5 bay leaves

2 teaspoons salt

½ cup ground piloncillo or brown sugar

Poke a hole or two in both sides of each chile. In a large skillet, sauté the onion and garlic in the oil until translucent but not browned. Add the chipotles and continue sautéing for 7 minutes, stirring constantly. Add all remaining ingredients. Continue sautéing until the chiles become very soft and pliable. Pour into a large glass container, allow to cool, then place in the refrigerator to marinate for two weeks. Serve sprinkled with a little Mexican oregano and a drizzle of olive oil.

MAKES ABOUT 6 CUPS

CHILES RELLENOS

STUFFED CHILES

There's nothing better than a good chile relleno and nothing worse than a bad one. This recipe reveals the secret for making great chiles rellenos every time.

15 poblano chiles

1 pound queso Oaxaca

All-purpose flour for dredging chiles

Corn oil for frying

8 eggs

½ teaspoon cream of tartar

Salt to taste

Without removing the stems, blister the chiles on the grill or under the broiler until all of the outsides are blistered and brown. Place the chiles in a plastic or paper bag and fold the bag down. Let the chiles stand for ten minutes and then peel them. Make a small slit in the side of each chile and put 1 to 2 tablespoons cheese inside. Dredge the chiles in flour.

In a large Dutch oven or deep, heavy iron frying pan, using a thermometer, heat the oil to 350 degrees.

Meanwhile, separate the eggs and lightly beat the yolks with a fork. In a food processor, beat the whites and the cream of tartar with a pinch of salt until very stiff. Gently fold in the beaten yolks with a rubber spatula.

Pick up one chile at a time by the stem, dip it in the egg batter, and very carefully set it in the hot oil (if you are not used to doing this next step, use tongs). Chiles will float on top of the oil. When golden brown, carefully turn them. When the other side is golden brown, they're done. Place them on paper towels to drain and salt them lightly. Serve immediately.

SERVES 15

JALAPEÑOS EN ESCABECHE

PICKLED JALAPEÑO CHILES

Pickled jalapeños are to Mexican food what crunchy dill pickles are is to the good old American cheeseburger. The removal of the seeds and veins makes this dish very mild.

1 ½ pounds jalapeño chiles, stems removed and rinsed

1 pound carrots, peeled and cut into ¼-inch rounds

3 tablespoons salt

½ cup corn oil

1 pound pearl onions, skins removed

4 cups white vinegar

10 cloves garlic, peeled

6 sprigs fresh thyme

½ teaspoon sugar

BLENDER

⅓ cup water

4 cloves garlic, minced

8 black peppercorns

1 teaspoon cumin seed

5 whole cloves

Pinch dried thyme

2 teaspoons Mexican oregano

10 bay leaves

MODERATE

GRINGO APPROVED

Cut the chiles into quarters lengthwise. Scrape out the seeds and veins (you may want to wear rubber gloves). Put the chiles and carrots in a large, glass mixing bowl and pour in the salt. Mix well and set aside for 1 hour.

Purée all blender ingredients well. Get the oil hot in a large frying pan; add blender ingredients and onions. Sauté the onions, stirring often, until translucent but not browned. Remove the chiles and carrots from the mixing bowl , with a slotted spoon, reserving the juice. Add chiles and carrots to the onions in the frying pan. Fry for 10 minutes more, stirring constantly. Add reserved juice and all other ingredients to the pan. Bring to a boil, then reduce heat and simmer for 8 minutes. Remove from heat and place in a large glass crock or bowl. Allow to cool. Cover and store in the refrigerator. Keeps in the refrigerator for about one week.

MAKES ½ GALLON

SOUPS AND BROTHS
SOPAS *y* CALDOS

I just bet that you, like myself, were brought up eating chicken noodle, vegetable beef, and tomato soup from that little red can; and furthermore, that the soup was served with the requisite grilled-cheese sandwich, only for lunch and always in the winter. When I asked my mom about this phenomenon, she told me, "We had five little kids, so every winter we found ourselves either eating soup to keep from getting colds or eating soup to get rid of colds. Besides, soup is cheap, quick, and easy." And that's the view that many of us, especially my generation, have of soup—it's an inexpensive, easy-to-make, wintertime cold remedy.

The Mexican view of soup is more European. In Mexico, soup is not something to have just now and then. It is made fresh and served daily, year-round, as a course before the entrée or, with some chopped white onion and cilantro and a little dried chile, as a stand-alone meal. Traditionally served as a starter for the main meal, which is served around mid-day, the flavors are subtle and soothing. And on the weekends, it is common to go out to little parlors specializing in soup after a night of dancing.

When it comes to Mexican soup, the everyday gringo thinks of menudo (which you'll find in the Mexican Breakfast chapter along with posole), but that's only a little part of the story. You won't believe the light, creamy flavor of Cream of Cilantro Soup, or if you're a fan of chicken soup, the delicate tangy flavor-twist in Sopa de Limón y Cilantro. In this chapter, you'll find some of my favorite authentic Mexican soup recipes. They are so easy and scrumptious that you may find yourself totally forgetting the little red can and making your own Mexican soups all the time.

SOPA DE TORTILLA

TORTILLA SOUP

My wife Kathy had a little café where the Tortilla Soup was always a local favorite. Although the café has been closed for years, every now and then we'll run into one of her old customers. They always remind us of how much they miss this delicious soup.

2 tablespoons corn oil

2 pounds pork shoulder, cut into ¾-inch cubes

1 white onion, finely chopped

2 cloves garlic, minced

12 Roma tomatoes

6 cups consomé de pollo (recipe page 45) or chicken broth

1 poblano chile, roasted, peeled, and chopped

1 jalapeño chile, seeded and minced

2 cloves garlic, minced

½ teaspoon ground cumin

1 teaspoon mild chile powder

¾ teaspoon black pepper

10 corn tortillas cut into very thin strips

GARNISH

Queso ranchero, chopped cilantro, finely chopped white onion, key lime wedges, and chiles tepinas

MODERATE

GRINGO APPROVED

In a large soup pot, sauté the pork until it starts to brown, then add the onions and garlic and continue sautéing until onions are starting to brown.

This next step may sound like a pain, but it just takes a few minutes and is well worth it. While pork is browning (or before), turn the tomatoes upside down and cut a 1-inch X across the bottom of each tomato, just through the skin. Fill a small saucepan with water and bring it to a boil. While the water is coming to a boil, fill a medium mixing bowl with ice and then add water to fill. Drop the tomatoes, one at a time, into the boiling water for 20 seconds. Remove from the boiling water with a slotted spoon and plunge into the ice-water bath. Using the edge of a paring knife, remove the core and skin. Cut the tomato in half from top to bottom and squeeze out all the seeds. Cut the tomatoes into ½-inch chunks. Add the tomatoes, consomé, poblano chile, jalapeño chile, garlic, and spices to the pork and onions. Bring to a boil and then reduce heat and simmer for 45 minutes.

Fill soup bowls about half full with tortilla strips and then ladle in soup to fill. Place garnishes in little bowls on the table, allowing your guests to garnish to their taste.

SERVES 6 TO 8

CONSOMÉ DE POLLO

CHICKEN BROTH

Just how authentic do you want your cooking? You could use canned chicken broth (and truth be told, I often do), but making your own is easy and the flavor is so much better that it will transcend your cooking to a new level. As your cooking skills increase, you will find yourself thinking ahead. Whenever you are cutting up a chicken, you save the scraps (neck, back, wing tips) in a bag in the freezer. When the bag gets full, you can substitute them for the whole chicken in this recipe.

(see recipes on pages 17, 33, 44, 47, 48, 59, 64, 111)

1 large chicken (about 4 pounds), including all giblets except liver

½ bunch flat-leaf parsley, chopped

1 white onion, skin on, chopped

1 small carrot, peeled, and sliced

2 cloves garlic

Salt to taste

5 black peppercorns

With a large cleaver, cut the chicken into pieces. Then cut the pieces in half, exposing the center of the bones. Place the chicken and all other ingredients in a large stock pot. Cover with about 3 inches of water. Bring to a low simmer and simmer, uncovered, for about 4 hours. From time to time, remove the froth from the top of the pot with a slotted spoon and discard. Remove from heat and allow to cool. Place in the refrigerator overnight to allow the flavor and gelatin to work out of the meat and bones. The next day, remove any fat that has risen to the top, discard, and reheat broth. Remove chicken and strain the broth. At this point, you may use immediately or pour the broth into ice cube trays and freeze. Once frozen, remove from trays and store in a plastic bag.

MAKES 10 CUPS

SOPA DE LIMÓN Y CILANTRO

CILANTRO LIME SOUP

This soup is zesty and delicious. I love to make up a big pot on a cold winter day—it's like taking Grandma's kitchen on a trip to Mexico.

2 tablespoons corn oil plus additional corn oil for frying tortilla wedges

1 poblano chile, roasted, peeled, and chopped

½ white onion, finely chopped

2 Roma tomatoes, chopped

6 cups consomé de pollo (recipe page 45) or chicken broth

1½ teaspoons key lime zest

2 key limes, juiced, and 1 sliced for garnish

3 tablespoons chopped, fresh cilantro

2½ pounds pollo deshebrado (recipe page 70)

Salt to taste

Freshly ground black pepper to taste

8 corn tortillas

Corn oil for frying

Freshly chopped cilantro for garnish

GRINGO FRIENDLY

In a large, heavy stockpot, sauté chile and onion in the corn oil. Stir in tomatoes and cook for 5 minutes. Add consomé, lime zest, lime juice, and 3 tablespoons fresh cilantro. Bring to a boil, then reduce heat and simmer, uncovered, for 20 minutes. Stir in chicken, salt, and pepper; simmer, uncovered, for 10 minutes.

Meanwhile, cut each tortilla into 8 wedges and fry in an inch of hot oil (350 degrees) until crisp. Drain on a paper towel and lightly salt. Place a few of the tortilla chips in each soup bowl and add soup.

Garnish with lime slices and cilantro.

MAKES 4 SERVINGS

OPPOSITE: *(clockwise from bottom) Sopa de Limón y Cilantro (recipe above), Crema de Cilantro con Tortillas (recipe page 48), and Sopa de Camarones (recipe page 49).*

CREMA DE CILANTRO CON TORTILLAS

CREAM OF CILANTRO SOUP WITH TORTILLA STRIPS

I got this recipe from a great little restaurant in Nogales, Mexico. It's light and creamy, and a great starter for an elegant dinner that you want to give a Mexican flare.

1 pound zucchini, chopped into ½-inch chunks

6 cups consomé de pollo (recipe page 45) or chicken broth

1 cup (tightly packed) cilantro, chopped

¼ cup salted butter

½ white onion, minced

1 clove garlic

2 tablespoons cornstarch

Corn oil for frying

4 corn tortillas

½ cup heavy cream

1 poblano chile, roasted, peeled, and diced

Salt and freshly ground black pepper to taste

½ pound queso blanco or any white Mexican cheese

GRINGO FRIENDLY

Simmer the zucchini for 20 minutes in lightly salted water and drain. Purée the zucchini and chicken broth in a blender, then add cilantro and purée again. In a large saucepan, sauté the onion and garlic in the butter until translucent, then add the mixture from the blender. Mix the cornstarch with a little cold water into a thin paste and add to the soup. Simmer for 15 minutes, stirring often.

Meanwhile, cut the tortillas into thin strips and deep fry, using a thermometer, in corn oil at 350 degrees until golden brown. Salt as soon as you take out of the oil and drain on paper towels.

Stir the cream and poblano into the soup, reduce heat, and let blend for 5 more minutes. Season and serve in big soup bowls with fried tortilla strips and a little queso blanco on top.

SERVES 6 TO 8

SOPA DE CAMARONES

SHRIMP SOUP

Down in Mexico, shrimp and soup are favorite traditions. This fantastic dish offers the best of both. Please note, this recipe calls for shrimp with the heads attached—the gringo line has been drawn in the sand, can you step across it?

4 tomatillos, husks removed, rinsed well, and cut into quarters

3 poblano chiles, seeds and veins removed, chopped

2 cups Italian parsley, rinsed well and chopped

3 leaves yerba santa (ask your grocer)

4 cups plus 2 tablespoons water

3 teaspoons corn oil

1 white onion, finely chopped

1½ tablespoons cornstarch

2 pounds medium shrimp with heads attached

½ teaspoon white pepper

Salt to taste

2 key limes, cut into wedges

Purée the tomatillos, poblanos, Italian parsley, yerba santa, and water in a blender. In a large saucepan, sauté the onion in the oil until tender. Add purée and bring to a light boil. Add 2 tablespoons water to the cornstarch and mix well. Add to the sopa and stir well. After the sopa thickens a little, add the shrimp and simmer, covered, for 5 minutes. Season to taste. Serve immediately in big soup bowls with a squeeze of key lime.

SERVES 6

49

SOPA DE ALBÓNDIGAS

MEATBALL SOUP

We go out for Mexican food with our friends Ryan and Claire at least once a month. Ryan always orders Albóndigas soup, so I wrote this easy, delicious recipe for him. Give it a try. Who knows, it might just end up being your favorite, too.

MEATBALLS

1 tablespoon long-grain rice

6 ounces ground beef

6 ounces ground pork

¼ medium white onion, finely minced

1 egg

½ teaspoon dried mint

½ teaspoon Mexican oregano

¼ teaspoon ground cumin

½ teaspoon freshly ground black pepper

Salt to taste

SOUP

3 Roma tomatoes

¼ medium white onion, minced

2 cloves garlic, minced

1 tablespoon corn oil

3 carrots, cleaned, peeled, and cut into ¼-inch rounds

2 small zucchini, cleaned, peeled, and cut into ¼-inch cubes

3 cups water

3 cups beef broth

1 güero chile, stems removed, and a slit cut in the side

2 tablespoons fresh cilantro, finely chopped

Put the rice in a little bowl or cup and cover with boiling water. Let the rice soak for 20 minutes. Mix all remaining meatball ingredients together well. Drain the rice and then work into the meat mixture. Roll into little meatballs an inch or so across.

Turn the tomatoes upside down and cut a 1-inch X across the bottom of each tomato, just through the skin. Fill a small saucepan with water and bring it to a boil. Drop the tomatoes, one at a time, into the boiling water for 20 seconds. Remove from the boiling water. Drop into a bowl of ice water and allow to cool. Using the edge of a paring knife, remove the core and skin. Cut in half from top to bottom, shake out the seeds, and dice. Set aside.

Purée the onion and garlic in a blender. In a large, hot stock pot, lightly simmer the mixture from the blender in the corn oil for 5 minutes or until slightly thickened and reduced. Add all other ingredients except meatballs. Bring to a simmer and then carefully add the meatballs. Simmer over very low heat for 1 hour, gently stirring now and then. If froth appears on top of the soup, remove with a slotted spoon and discard. When the vegetables are soft and the meatballs well cooked, serve with wedges of key lime.

SERVES 5 TO 6

CALDO DE MARISCOS

SEAFOOD SOUP

If I walk into a Mexican restaurant and they have beef Chimichangas with sour cream on the menu but no Caldo de Mariscos, I might walk right back out the door. If you like seafood, this soup is fantastic, and it's real Mexico!

6 plum tomatoes, chopped

½ white onion, chopped

3 cloves garlic, finely chopped

⅓ cup olive oil

½ teaspoon Mexican oregano

⅛ teaspoon ground cumin

Salt to taste

½ teaspoon black pepper

2½ quarts fish stock

2 dozen medium shrimp, peeled and deveined

1½ pounds red snapper, cut into chunks

8 large crab claws

Key lime wedges for garnish

Jalapeño chile strips for garnish

MODERATE

GRINGO APPROVED

Purée the tomatoes, onion, and garlic in a blender. In a stockpot, heat the olive oil and add the tomato mixture. Cook over medium-low heat until thickened, stirring often. Add the oregano, cumin, salt, pepper, and fish stock, and bring to a boil over a medium-low heat for 10 minutes. Add the shrimp, fish, and crab claws, and continue cooking for another 10 minutes. Serve immediately.

Garnish with fresh key lime wedges and strips of jalapeño chile on the side.

SERVES 8

The big companies in the good old U.S. of A. that make the national brands of salsa know as much about good salsa (and Mexican food in general) as a cow knows about dancing. Comparing bottled salsa with fresh homemade salsa is like comparing prime rib with those little canned cocktail sausages. The reason these salsas are not very flavorful is that they are kept fresh with chemical preservatives, and the result is sort of a jalapeño-flavored tomato sauce. If the salsa had any subtle flavors to begin with, after being on the shelf a short while, they will have all vanished.

SAUCES
SALSAS

On the other hand, salsa in Mexico is a centuries-old culinary art form with a hundred (or more) different flavors and uses. As with any great cuisine, these sauces are the heart of the meal. Authentic Mexican salsa is sometimes very hot, but not always. Unlike their counterparts from the U.S., they are so much more than just a way to add heat. The flavors are complex, full-bodied, well-balanced, and, like a fine wine, they complement a meal rather than overpower it.

Making your own salsa, like Grandma's apple pie, is a labor of love. You need to smell the chiles roasting and taste the spices as you go. Start out making my personal favorite, Guadalajaran Salsa en Molcajete, and you'll never go back to the bottled stuff. And salsas aren't just for chips and nachos. Take an ordinary grilled chicken and serve it with tangy, spicy Tomatillo Salsa Verde or Salsa de Pipián con Chile Güero, with its unexpected fiery flavor, and suddenly you're serving a real Mexican treat. Add a few extras like Mexican rice, warm corn tortillas, and an ice-cold Mexican beer, and you'll have a full-blown fiesta on your hands.

GUADALAJARAN SALSA EN MOLCAJETE

GUADALAJARAN SALSA MADE IN A MOLCAJETE

You'll find this distinctive salsa made tableside at fine restaurants in Guadalajara. A molcajete is a centuries-old kitchen tool, sort of the Aztec version of the mortar and pestle (see photo below).

3 pulla chiles

4 tomatillos

3 Roma tomatoes

1 teaspoon coarse sea salt

1 clove garlic, minced

¼ white onion, finely chopped

⅓ bunch cilantro, chopped

Toast the chiles on a hot, dry comal for 2 or 3 minutes, turning often to avoid burning. Turn heat up. Remove the cores from the tomatillos and tomatoes and then char the outsides on the comal until dark brown or lightly blackened. Coarsely chop the tomatillos and tomatoes and set aside.

Place the salt and then the garlic in the bottom of the molcajete. Work into a paste. Add the chiles and break up into small pieces. Add the tomatillos and tomatoes, working into mixture. Now add the onion and cilantro, but stir in—do not grind. Serve with tortilla chips.

MAKES 2 CUPS

SALSA PARA MARISCOS

SALSA FOR SEAFOOD

The little fish taco stands along the Sea of Cortez in Mexico use this salsa to give their tacos that special taste. The secret is the cucumber. It goes well with any fish.

4 to 6 large, ripe tomatoes, diced

1 large cucumber, peeled, seeds removed, and chopped

2 jalapeño chiles, stems removed, and chopped

1 large white onion, chopped

1 bunch cilantro, cleaned and chopped

At least 2 teaspoons salt (I know it looks like a lot,

but for the right flavor, it takes more than you would think.)

GRINGO
BEWARE

Place all ingredients in a large bowl and allow flavors to blend for about ½ hour before serving.

MAKES 4 CUPS

SALSA DE TOMATILLO Y AGUACATE

AVOCADO AND TOMATILLO SALSA

This delicious salsa is a step up from guacamole. It's fantastic with chips, but I always serve it with flautas. It makes my guests go crazy.

6 tomatillos, husked and rinsed well

½ white onion, chopped

½ bunch cilantro, chopped

1 clove garlic, minced

1 serrano chile, stem removed

2 tablespoons water

1 teaspoon salt

1 ripe Haas avocado, peeled and cubed

GRINGO
APPROVED

Place tomatillos, onion, cilantro, garlic, chile, water, and salt in a blender; purée until smooth. Add avocado and purée until smooth. Add more water if needed—salsa should be a little thicker than tomato sauce.

MAKES 3 CUPS

SALSA BORRACHA

DRUNKEN SALSA

The use of beer and tequila in salsa is very common all over Mexico. This salsa is a good one for vegetarians who don't mind a little beer. It is fabulous with chips, Mexican rice, and refried beans.

2 large, ripe tomatoes

1 small white onion, sliced into ½-inch slices

3 jalapeño chiles

2 large cloves garlic, unpeeled

¼ teaspoon Mexican oregano, toasted

¼ teaspoon cumin

½ cup Tecate beer

Salt to taste

GRINGO
BEWARE

Roast the tomatoes, onion slices, chiles, and garlic on a comal until dark brown and well blistered. Remove from comal and peel the garlic. Coarsely chop, mix well in a bowl, and add spices and beer. Salt mixture again and allow flavors to blend for 30 minutes before serving.

MAKES 3 TO 4 CUPS

SALSA DE TOMATILLO ASADO Y CHILE DE ARBOL

CHARRED TOMATILLO AND CHILE DE ARBOL SALSA

This is a step farther away from gringo territory. This salsa is fantastic on tacos and chips, or anywhere you want a little fire!

8 tomatillos, peeled and rinsed well

8 chiles de arboles

½ teaspoon corn oil

3 cloves garlic

1 teaspoon kosher salt

½ teaspoon Mexican oregano

½ teaspoon piloncillo or brown sugar

DANGER
GRINGO KILLER

Place tomatillos on a comal over medium-high heat; blister the outside and remove from comal. Toast chiles, shaking back and forth in hot comal until lightly browned, about 45 seconds. Lightly oil the comal and toast the garlic until browned. Peel garlic and place all ingredients in a blender. Purée until smooth.

MAKES 2 CUPS

58

SALSA COLORADA PARA ENCHILADAS

RED SAUCE FOR ENCHILADAS

If your enchilada experience is based around canned enchilada sauce, you won't believe the rich and yet delicate flavor of this homemade sauce. It's a little more work to make your own enchilada sauce from scratch, but well worth the effort.

10 to 12 dried colorado chiles

4 cups consomé de pollo (recipe page 45) or chicken broth

2 cloves garlic, minced

1 teaspoon dried Mexican oregano

½ teaspoon ground cumin

½ teaspoon salt

½ teaspoon piloncillo, ground

MODERATE

GRINGO APPROVED

Toast the chiles on a hot, dry comal until soft and pliable. Remove chiles from comal and allow to cool a little. Remove and discard the stems and seeds. Place all ingredients in a saucepan and simmer for 15 minutes. Pour into a blender, ½ cup at a time, and purée. (Be careful—hot liquids expand in a blender and can spill out of the top and burn you.)

Pour the sauce through a sieve into a bowl, mashing with the back of a spoon, until only the chile solids are left in the sieve. Discard solids. If sauce is too thin, place back in saucepan and reduce to about the consistency of a thick tomato sauce. Serve sauce warm.

MAKES 4½ CUPS

SALSA DE CHILE GUAJILLO PARA ENCHILADAS

GUAJILLO CHILE ENCHILADA SAUCE

Make this easy sauce and your gringo days will soon be over. The slightly sweet, mildly hot flavor of guajillo chiles goes well with roast pork.

15 dried guajillo chiles

3 cups beef broth

3 cloves garlic, minced

2 teaspoons piloncillo, ground, or brown sugar

1 teaspoon Mexican oregano

½ teaspoon ground cumin

½ teaspoon kosher salt

MODERATE

GRINGO APPROVED

Toast the chiles on a hot, dry comal until soft and pliable. Remove chiles from comal and allow to cool a little. Remove stems and seeds. Place all ingredients in a saucepan and simmer for 15 minutes. Pour into a blender, ½ a cup at a time, and purée. (Be careful—hot liquids expand in a blender and can spill out of the top and burn you.)

Pour the sauce through a sieve into a bowl, mashing with the back of a spoon, until only the chile solids are left in the sieve. Discard chile solids. If sauce is too thin, place back in saucepan and reduce to about the consistency of a thick tomato sauce. Serve warm.

MAKES 3½ CUPS

OPPOSITE: *(clockwise from bottom) Salsa Colorada para Enchiladas (recipe page 59), Salsa de Chile Guajillo para Enchiladas (recipe above), and Guacamole (recipe page 62).*

GUACAMOLE

GUACAMOLE

I learned about guacamole from my Uncle Jack and Aunt Pat. They had an avocado orchard, and when the avocados were ripe, we ate them with everything. The secret to good guacamole is to fold the ingredients together, not mash it into a paste.

2 ripe Haas avocados, peeled, seeded, and chopped into ¾-inch chunks

½ white onion, finely chopped

1 Roma tomato, chopped

1 jalapeño chile, finely chopped

2 cloves garlic, minced

Juice of 1 key lime

Celery salt to taste

Freshly ground black pepper to taste

MODERATE

GRINGO
APPROVED

Gently fold all ingredients together. Serve with tortilla chips and ice-cold margaritas!

MAKES 3 CUPS

MOLE DE QUATRO CHILES

FOUR CHILE SAUCE

This is an easy place for the average cook to start making mole. The use of four different chiles gives this sauce a unique depth of flavor.

8 dried guajillo chiles

3 mild New Mexico chiles

3 pasilla chiles

2 ancho chiles

4 cups beef broth

3 cloves garlic, minced

2 teaspoons piloncillo, ground, or brown sugar

1 teaspoon Mexican oregano

½ teaspoon ground cumin

½ teaspoon salt

¼ teaspoon ground canela

½ ounce bittersweet chocolate

Roast the chiles on a hot, dry comal until soft and pliable. Remove chiles from comal and allow to cool a little. Remove stems and seeds. Place all ingredients in a saucepan and simmer for 15 minutes. Pour into a blender, ½ cup at a time, and purée. (Be careful—hot liquids expand in a blender and can spill out of the top and burn you.)

Pour the sauce through a sieve into a bowl, mashing with the back of a spoon, until only the chile solids are left. Discard chile solids. If sauce is too thin, return to heat and thicken. Serve warm with enchiladas or any grilled meat or poultry.

MAKES 5 CUPS

SALSA DE TOMATILLO VERDE

GREEN TOMATILLO SALSA

This tart sauce is a must for Huevos Rancheros. It's also delicious on enchiladas, green corn tamales, and grilled fish, chicken, or pork.

1 pound tomatillos, husks removed and washed

1 jalapeño chile

2 cloves garlic, chopped

1 tablespoon corn oil

⅓ cup consomé de pollo (recipe page 45) or chicken broth

Salt to taste

GRINGO
FRIENDLY

In a medium saucepan, barely cover the tomatillos and chile with water and simmer for 8 minutes or until tomatillos turn soft. Transfer tomatillos, chile, and ¼ cup of the cooking water to a blender; add garlic and blend until smooth. In a large heavy frying pan over medium heat, heat oil; add sauce from blender and simmer for 5 minutes, stirring occasionally. Add broth; continue to cook for 5 minutes more. Salt to taste.

MAKES ABOUT 2 CUPS

SALSA DE PIPIÁN Y CHILE GÜERO

PUMPKIN SEED AND YELLOW HOT CHILE SALSA

I like to think of this one as "ugly salsa." It is not appealing to the eye, but it has a great flavor and goes well with grilled seafood, and especially lobster.

1 to 2 teaspoons corn oil

3 güero chiles

1 white onion, thickly sliced

2 tomatoes

½ bulb garlic

⅓ cup pumpkin seeds, shelled

1 cup water

½ teaspoon salt

¼ teaspoon Mexican oregano

GRINGO BEWARE

Toast the chiles, onion, tomatoes, and garlic on a lightly oiled (about 1 teaspoon) comal or iron frying pan until lightly charred and toasted brown. Remove the seeds and stems from the chiles. Squeeze the garlic out of the bulb; set aside.

Re-oil the comal or frying pan lightly and toast the pumpkin seeds until browned and puffed up.

Place all ingredients in a food processor and purée until a coarse salsa is formed.

MAKES 2½ CUPS

SALSA CRUDA

RAW SALSA

This easy salsa should be in every cook's arsenal for authentic Mexican cooking. Try it with tortilla chips and an ice-cold margarita.

3 serrano chiles, diced

½ white onion, diced

3 large ripe plum tomatoes, diced

½ bunch fresh cilantro, chopped

2 teaspoons corn oil

½ teaspoon salt

Juice of ½ key lime

Mix all ingredients together and let stand 1 hour to blend.

MAKES 2½ CUPS

SALSA DE LA CASA

HOUSE SALSA

This is the hot sauce traditionally served with tacos in northern Mexico. It's a good, basic hot sauce that tastes great with chips.

1 (8-ounce) can tomato sauce

2 teaspoons crushed red chiles

1 teaspoon whole Mexican oregano

¼ teaspoon salt

Mix all ingredients and let stand. This sauce keeps about a week in the refrigerator.

MAKES 1 CUP

SALSA RANCHERA

RANCH-STYLE SALSA

The use of chipotle chiles and adobo sauce in this salsa makes it fantastic with Mexican breakfasts, and I also like adding a little to my homemade barbecue sauce.

1 teaspoon corn oil

6 tomatillos, husked and rinsed

6 cloves garlic (do not remove peel)

1 medium white onion, diced

3 canned chipotle chiles

1 tablespoon adobo sauce from the can of chipotles

½ bunch fresh cilantro, chopped

1 cup hot water

½ teaspoon salt

GRINGO APPROVED

In a large heavy skillet, brown the tomatillos in the corn oil. Remove tomatillos from skillet and then brown the garlic and onions. Peel garlic and place all ingredients in a blender. Blend on high until smooth. Serve warm. Keeps for 2 or 3 days in the refrigerator.

MAKES 2 CUPS

MAIN COURSES
PLATOS PRINCIPALES

It's great when you learn one thing

that can be used in several different ways, and even bet-

ter when you learn ten things that can be used in a hundred. That's

the beauty of Mexican cooking. When your family goes to a good Mexican

food restaurant on either side of the border, dinner often goes something like this:

Dad orders his favorite, the #2, which is a chile relleno and two chicken tacos with rice

and beans. For Mom, it's one chicken enchilada with rice, and Daughter, being a picky eater,

orders a chicken flauta, a la carte, with guacamole on the side.

Here's the thing. All three entrées are made using one common ingredient—*pollo deshebrado*

(poached chicken), which was cooked earlier. The cook stuffs some of the poached chicken into

tortillas for Dad's tacos, then adds a few ingredients to the same chicken for Mom's enchilada and

Daughter's flauta, cooks them up in a deep fryer or broiler, and voila! The waitress is saying, "Careful,

the plate is hot," before Dad has finished his margarita.

Likewise, in the personal home kitchens in Mexico, many basic recipes such as Carnitas or Ropa

Vieja are used in tamales, tacos, enchiladas, and burritos, just to name a few.

This chapter will help you to say goodbye to tacos made from hamburger fried with that

envelope of taco seasoning and topped with cheddar cheese, and will be the basis for your

transformation out of the realm of gringo-style Mexican cooking forever! Once you've

mastered these simple, basic recipes (and you will), you'll go on to make all of

your favorite Mexican dishes. The recipes are simple and so delicious

that when you ask the family where they want to go for Mexican

dinner, they'll say, "Let's stay home," because yours

is the best in town!

POLLO DESHEBRADO

POACHED CHICKEN

This is the basic chicken used in tacos, enchiladas, burritos, and so on. I like to make this when I am already making chicken soup. Then, for the next few days, my family and I snack on chicken tacos, enchiladas, or flautas. *(see recipes on pages 47, 86, 89, 98)*

4 whole chicken breasts with skin and bone
Consomé de pollo (recipe page 45) or chicken broth to cover

Cut each of the chicken breasts into 4 pieces, exposing the bone. In a large stock pot, bring the chicken and consomé to a light simmer. Simmer for about 25 minutes or until just tender. Do not overcook. Remove from heat and allow the chicken to fully cool down in the broth. Once cool, strain and save the broth for soup or sauce. Remove the meat from the bones and shred. Discard the bones and cut up a little of the skin and add to the shredded chicken. This adds flavor and keeps the chicken moist.

MAKES ABOUT 1 POUND

CHILE VERDE

GREEN CHILE

This is a big favorite around my neighborhood. I usually make it on a cold winter night when we're sitting by the fire. I serve it in big soup bowls with cornbread right out of the oven. *(see recipe on page 96)*

RUB

1 tablespoon kosher salt

1 tablespoon piloncillo, ground, or
brown sugar

2 teaspoons freshly ground black pepper

2 teaspoons granulated garlic

1 teaspoon ground cayenne pepper

4 pounds pork rump roast

1 tablespoon corn oil

1 white onion, chopped

4 cloves fresh garlic, minced

4 medium white potatoes, cut into ½-inch cubes

1 (48-ounce can) chicken broth or
consomé de pollo (recipe page 45)

2 (14½-ounce) cans diced tomatoes

2 pounds poblano chiles, roasted and peeled

1 pound Anaheim chiles, roasted and peeled

2 teaspoons Mexican oregano

1 tablespoon ground cumin

Salt to taste

Black pepper to taste

GRINGO
BEWARE

Mix the rub ingredients together. Rub into the exterior of the roast. Place in a 375-degree oven for about two hours or until roast reaches an internal temperature of 165 degrees. Remove from oven and allow to cool. Cut into bite-size pieces, removing and discarding any fat; set meat aside.

In a large Dutch oven, brown the onion and garlic in the corn oil. Add potatoes, chicken broth, and tomatoes. Bring to a boil, reduce heat, and simmer for ten minutes. Add the pork and both green chiles and simmer for about 1 hour. Add oregano and cumin; season with salt and pepper to taste. If stew gets too thick while cooking, add a little water. Stir often.

SERVES 8 TO 10

CHILE COLORADO

MEXICAN RED CHILE

This Mexican version of a big warm bowl of hot stew on a cold day is fantastic when served with fresh, hot corn tortillas, and even better the next day in a burrito. *(see recipe on page 97)*

18 mild red chile pods

1 quart boiling water

2 cloves garlic

1 teaspoon salt

1 teaspoon Mexican oregano

½ teaspoon ground cumin

¼ cup corn oil

1 (4- to 5-pound) pork shoulder, cut into 1-inch cubes

¼ cup flour

¾ cups chicken broth

MODERATE

GRINGO APPROVED

Preheat the oven to 250 degrees. Remove the stems and seeds from the chiles. Place the chiles on a cookie sheet and bake in the oven for 3 minutes, turning often to avoid burning, or toast on a warm comal. Place the chiles in a large mixing bowl and cover with boiling water. Let stand for 10 to 12 minutes. Run the chiles a few at a time through the blender with a little of the soaking water until blended to a smooth paste. Repeat this process until all of the chiles and water are used, but in the last blending add the garlic, salt, oregano, and cumin. Set aside.

In a large Dutch oven, heat the oil. Dredge the pork in the flour. Fry the pork over medium heat, turning often until all sides are browned. Add the chicken broth and simmer for 8 to 10 minutes. Reduce heat, add red chile sauce, stir well, and cover. Simmer for 30 to 45 minutes, until the pork is quite tender.

SERVES 6

BISTEC RANCHERO

RANCH-STYLE STEAK

My daughter Katie taught us this recipe after she spent some time in a little pueblo just out of Magdalena de Kino. It's quick, easy, and a true treat from northern Mexico.

1 tablespoon salt

½ tablespoon black pepper

1 pound breakfast steak (round steaks thinly sliced)

2 tablespoons corn oil

1 white onion, thinly sliced

2 cloves garlic, minced

1 pound white potatoes, washed and thinly sliced

2 beefsteak tomatoes, thinly sliced

A few sprigs cilantro, finely chopped

GRINGO
FRIENDLY

Mix together the salt and pepper. Rub generously into the exterior of the steaks and shake off excess. Pour the oil into a large, heavy, unheated, skillet. Layer all of the onion, then the garlic, then the potatoes, then the tomato and cilantro, and finally the beef into the skillet. It is important that the steaks do not overlap, and never do two layers. (If cooking for a large group, do this in batches.)

Cover skillet, place on burner and turn heat to medium. Slow-cook without stirring until beef is fully cooked and potatoes are tender. Serve with hot corn tortillas, Jalapeños en Escabeche (recipe page 41), and refried beans. Yummm!

SERVES 6

MACHACA

DRIED, SHREDDED MEAT

Machaca roughly means dried, shredded meat. It is sold in the markets of Mexico in plastic bags and looks like finely shredded beef jerky. The original recipe calls for drying the beef in the sun and then pounding it with a stone. This recipe is a little more "gringo friendly." Many so-called Mexican-food restaurants in the U.S. sell shredded beef for machaca. My neighbor Darryl is annoyed to no end by this deceit. True machaca has a complex, smoky flavor, and once you've had the real thing, you'll never look at shredded beef the same way again. My recipe calls for tomato, which many say is not authentic, and rightly so, but I've been served it both ways in Mexico, so you choose. Either way, it's delicious. *(see recipes on pages 16, 94, 100)*

2 pounds round steak, cubed

1 tablespoon kosher salt

Pure mesquite charcoal

½ cup corn oil

1 white onion, finely chopped

2 cloves garlic, minced

2 Roma tomatoes, finely chopped

2 poblano chiles, roasted, peeled, and chopped

Rub the meat well with the salt and then spread out in a large baking dish. Slow-smoke the meat in the upper chamber of a smoker at 275 degrees for 3 hours or until meat is fully dried out. You may also do this in your oven but you will lose the smoky flavor. A little at a time, shred the dried beef in a food processor until fine. At this point the machaca can be stored in a plastic bag in the freezer for a long time.

When you're ready to serve the machaca, sauté the onions and garlic in the oil until translucent and add the machaca and all other ingredients. Fry until the tomatoes are fully cooked. You may want to taste for salt level. Serve immediately with fresh hot tortillas and Salsa de la Casa (recipe page 66).

SERVES 6 TO 8

CARNE ASADA

GRILLED MEAT

My family and I attended the wedding of my friend Santiago's daughter in the village of Terrenate, in northern Mexico. The cooking went on for two days and included butchering and cooking a whole cow. Several hundred people from the surrounding pueblos showed up on the second day for the fiesta. But on the first night, Santiago made Carne Asada Tacos for the thirty-some friends who showed up to help with the preparations. Carne asada can be used in tacos, burritos, or served with warm tortillas. *(see recipe on page 84)*

Pure mesquite charcoal (not briquettes)

1 (1-pound) skirt steak

Salt

Pepper

½ teaspoon Mexican oregano

Place the charcoal in the grill and light. Once the coals are glowing red, toss the skirt steak on the grill and lightly salt and pepper the side facing up. Turn the steak when the first side is nice and brown. Salt, pepper, and sprinkle the oregano on the browned side. Grill to medium and remove from heat. Before using or serving, cut into little strips across the grain.

MAKES A LITTLE LESS THAN 1 POUND

ROPA VIEJA

SHREDDED BEEF

Ropa Vieja means "old clothes," but it refers to using leftover roast or stewed meat with vegetables for tacos, burritos, tostadas, and so on. The recipe tells you how to start from scratch, but remember this idea the next time you have some leftover roast beef! *(see recipes on pages 83, 89)*

1- to 2-pound chuck roast

1 tablespoon red wine vinegar

Salt to taste

Freshly ground black pepper

2 teaspoons corn oil

2 cloves garlic, finely minced

½ white onion, diced

1 chopped tomato

2 roasted poblano chiles, peeled and diced

1 serrano chile, finely chopped

½ teaspoon Mexican oregano

Preheat the oven to 300 degrees. Place the roast in a heavy roasting pan. Sprinkle the vinegar over the roast and season with salt and pepper.

Slow roast for 1½ hours. Remove roast from heat and allow to cool. Depending on how tender the roast is, either shred the roast with a fork or cut it into strips and then shred by hand.

Heat the oil in a large sauté pan and cook the onions and garlic until they are soft. Add the beef and then stir in all other ingredients. Cook for 5 more minutes.

MAKES ABOUT 2½ POUNDS

CARNITAS

LITTLE MEATS

Carnitas are delicious. We serve them with charro beans, salsa, and tortillas. We use the leftovers for tacos or green or red chile, and they are out of this world fried and served with Huevos Rancheros.

(see recipes on pages 83, 89, 91)

RUB

1 tablespoon kosher salt

1 tablespoon piloncillo, ground, or brown sugar

2 teaspoons freshly ground black pepper

2 teaspoons granulated garlic

1 teaspoon pasilla chile powder

1 teaspoon Mexican oregano

4 pounds pork rump roast

MODERATE

GRINGO
APPROVED

Mix the rub ingredients together. Rub into the exterior of the roast. Let rest for 30 minutes. Place in roasting pan in the oven at 375 degrees for about 1 ½ hours or until roast reaches an internal temperature of 165 degrees. Remove from oven and allow to cool. Cut into bite-size pieces, removing any fat.

MAKES ABOUT 3 POUNDS

KATIE'S TACO MEAT

My daughter Katie learned Spanish at the age of 8 from the little Mexican girls next door. She spent many an afternoon at their house, playing, talking, and cooking. She brought this recipe home and made it for us when she was 11 or 12. It's a family favorite, and it'll be the best taco salad you've ever eaten.

½ white onion, minced

2 cloves garlic

4 tomatoes, diced

1 large bunch cilantro

2 pounds ground beef

1 pound breakfast steaks (round steak thinly sliced), sliced into little strips

Salt to taste

Corn tortillas, warmed

GARNISH

Shredded green cabbage, finely chopped white onion,
avocado slices, crumbled queso Ranchero, key lime wedges, and chiles tepinas

GRINGO
FRIENDLY

Place the onion, garlic, and tomatoes in a skillet and start sautéing. As soon as the tomatoes give off their liquid, add all other ingredients. Cook until the meat is done. Serve with warm corn tortillas and garnishes.

SERVES 4

CARNE ADOBADA

MARINATED MEAT

This flavorful dish is Mexico's version of barbecued pork. The taste is good old all-American barbecued pork wearing a sombero.

24 guajillo chile pods

6 cups consomé de pollo (recipe page 45) or chicken broth

4 cloves garlic, minced

2 teaspoons Mexican oregano

½ teaspoon ground chile de arbol or cayenne

1 teaspoon salt

1 (4-pound) boneless pork shoulder, fat trimmed and cut into large chunks

MODERATE

GRINGO APPROVED

Toast the chile pods on a dry comal or iron frying pan until dark brown but not burnt (if the chiles burn they will become bitter). Remove stems, seeds, and veins. Break the chiles up and simmer in the chicken broth along with the garlic, oregano, chile de arbol, and salt for 20 minutes. Run chiles and broth through the blender ½ cup at a time. (Be careful—hot liquids expand in a blender and can spill out of the top and burn you.)

Pour the sauce through a sieve into a bowl, working sauce through the sieve with the back of a spoon, until only the chile solids are left in the sieve. Discard chile solids.

Pour sauce over pork in a large, heavy Dutch oven or baking dish with a lid. Bake, covered, at 350 degrees for 1½ hours. Remove from oven, let cool enough to handle, shred with two forks and mix back into sauce. Serve with hot corn tortillas and an ice-cold Mexican beer.

MAKES ABOUT 3 POUNDS

MOLE NEGRO OAXAQUEÑO

OAXACAN BLACK MOLE

This famous dish is considered the king of all moles. It is traditionally served on "The Day of the Dead." Yes, it's a little work. So put on a little "Música Tropical," ice down a few Negra Modelos, and do as they do in Mexico—have a few good friends over and put everybody to work: someone toasting chiles, someone cutting and then cooking the chicken, someone measuring ingredients, and so on. It's not work, it's a mole-making fiesta.

2 roasting chickens	¼ cup raw almonds	1 tablespoon pecans
6½ quarts water	2 tablespoons raw peanuts, skinned	5 plum tomatoes, chopped
2 chiles de arboles	1 stick canela, about 1 inch long	4 medium tomatillos, chopped
½ teaspoon dried, ground thyme	4 black peppercorns	1 sprig fresh thyme
2 whole allspice	3 whole cloves	½ teaspoon Mexican oregano
1½ tablespoons salt	6 tablespoons corn oil plus some for	1 medium white onion, quartered
1 teaspoon freshly ground black pepper	lightly oiling comal	8 cloves garlic
5 negro chiles	1 tablespoon bacon drippings	1 avocado leaf
5 guajillo chiles	1½ tablespoons raisins	4½ ounces Ibarra chocolate,
5 ancho chiles	1 slice egg bread	broken into small pieces
5 mulato chiles	1 small ripe plantain, cut into slices	Salt to taste
2 chipotle chiles	½ cup sesame seeds	

Cut the chickens into leg, thigh, wing, and breast pieces. Remove the skin but save along with the backs, necks, and giblets. In a large stock pot, bring 5 quarts of water to a boil. Add the chicken (including the skin, giblets, necks, and backs), chiles de arboles, thyme, allspice, salt, and freshly ground black pepper. Reduce heat and simmer for 30 to 45 minutes or until the chicken juice runs clear when pierced. Remove pieces of chicken. Strain stock and discard spices, skin, giblets, necks, and backs.

While chicken is simmering, remove all remaining dried chile stems and veins and discard, but save the seeds. Toast all the chiles on a dry comal or iron frying pan until dark brown but not until burnt (if the chiles burn they will become bitter).

Place all the toasted chiles in a large bowl and cover with 1½ quarts of boiling water. Soak for 20 minutes. Remove the chiles from the water and run them through the blender a few at a time, with just enough of the soaking water to purée them to the consistency of a thin ketchup. (Be careful—hot liquids expand in a blender and can spill out of the top and burn you.) Pour the sauce through a sieve into a bowl, working sauce through the sieve with the back of a spoon, until only the chile solids are left. Discard chile solids. Set sauce aside.

Meanwhile, (I like to do this next step outside), on a dry comal or iron frying pan, toast the almonds, peanuts, canela, black peppercorns, and cloves—be careful not to burn. Set aside. Reduce heat and toast the seeds that you saved from the dried chiles until just blackened—be careful not to burn, and watch out—the smoke is very intense. Remove comal from heat, push the seeds together, light with a match, and allow to burn out. Place the blackened seeds in a cup of cold water and let soak for 10 minutes. While seeds are soaking, lightly oil the comal and sauté the onion and garlic until lightly browned. Set aside. Drain the blackened seeds and set aside.

In a deep, heavy iron frying pan, heat 3 tablespoons corn oil and bacon drippings until very hot. Fry the raisins for 1 minute and remove from pan, leaving the oil. Set aside. Fry the slice of bread until brown and remove from pan, leaving the oil. Set aside. In the same pan over medium heat, fry the plantain slices until browned. Set aside. Reduce heat and toast the sesame seeds until they start to turn color. Add the pecans and toast 2 minutes more, stirring constantly. Remove from heat and allow to cool. Grind to a fine powder in a spice grinder. Set aside. Place the blackened seeds in the spice grinder and grind to a powder. Add blackened seed powder to the chile sauce and stir well.

In the frying pan, cook the tomatoes, tomatillos, thyme, and oregano until most of the juices evaporate. Add ½ cup of chicken stock, stir well, and remove from heat. Set aside.

In a blender, purée the almonds, peanuts, canela, black peppercorns, cloves, raisins, bread, plantain, ground sesame seeds and pecans, 2 cups of the chicken stock, and onions and garlic until smooth .

Okay, this is the part you've waited for. In a large stock pot, heat remaining 3 tablespoons corn oil until very hot. Reduce heat to medium low and fry the chile sauce until almost dry, stirring constantly. Don't let it burn. Add tomato mixture and fry until most of the liquid has evaporated. Add mixture from blender and 1 cup of chicken stock and stir well. Simmer for 30 minutes, stirring often.

Toast the avocado leaf and add to the pot along with the chocolate. Keep simmering and adding chicken stock as needed for 30 more minutes. Mole should be thick enough to just coat the back of a spoon. Taste mole and adjust salt level. In a separate pot, simmer the chicken pieces in remaining chicken stock until hot. Place 1 piece of chicken in a shallow bowl and spoon on enough mole to totally cover. Serve with fresh, hot corn tortillas.

SERVES 10

I was shopping at the mall with a friend who was staying with me from Mexico. At a "Mexican" restaurant in the food court, he ordered "Beef Tacos." The plate had two U-shaped, corn chip-like taco shells stuffed with hamburger and then lettuce, tomato, and shredded yellow cheese. On the side were those little packets of "hot sauce." After he was done eating, I asked him what he thought. He said, "They don't make tacos like that anywhere in Mexico that I've been." Then he teased me, saying, "Now I know why you gringos think Mexican food is so greasy."

TACOS AND TAMALES
TACOS *y* TAMALES

When I'm in Mexico, one of my favorite treats is going to the little taco stands. Inland they make several different meat tacos cooked over mesquite charcoal. They come with hand-made tortillas, grilled spring onions, and large, red radishes. To top it off, they are drizzled with fresh-squeezed lime juice and smoking-hot, homemade salsa. By the sea, it's fish and shrimp tacos topped with cabbage, white onion, and cilantro. Both are served with Mexican beer so cold it almost hurts your teeth.

In this chapter, you'll learn about tacos and tamales. There are so many varieties of both, I could do an entire book on either one. Tacos have dozens of different fillings and just as many toppings and salsas. Likewise, tamales have dozens of different wrappers, and the fillings include everything from fish, chiles, and fruit to beef, poultry, and even iguana (yes, that big lizard). I've included several of my favorite easy, authentic taco and tamale recipes. Try them all; you'll find they are well worth the time.

TACOS DE RES

BEEF TACOS

This is your basic shredded beef taco, and most likely the first taco most of us try in the United States. They're easy to make and delicious.

1 pound Ropa Vieja (recipe page 76)

12 corn tortillas, warmed on a comal or frying pan

Corn oil for frying

Shredded lettuce

½ pound queso Ranchero, crumbled

Salsa de la Casa (recipe page 66)

Place 2 to 3 tablespoons of Ropa Vieja in each tortilla and fold closed. Using tongs to hold the tortilla closed, fry each taco in the oil until crisp. Place on a paper towel to drain; salt immediately. Top each taco with lettuce and a little queso Ranchero. Serve with Salsa de la Casa.

SERVES 6

TACOS DE CARNITAS

TACOS WITH LITTLE MEATS

For the average gringo, trying Tacos de Carnitas for the first time takes them a step farther south. I just love these things.

12 corn tortillas, warmed on a comal or frying pan

1 pound carnitas (recipe page 77)

½ white onion, minced

½ bunch cilantro, finely chopped

6 key lime wedges

6 chiles tepinas

Place two tortillas, one on top of the other, on each plates. Place 3 tablespoons of carnitas in the center of each tortilla. Top with onion and cilantro and set 1 lime wedge and 1 chile tepín on the side of each plate.

SERVES 6

TACOS DE CARNE ASADA

GRILLED BEEF TACOS

These are my favorite tacos. You'll find them served all over northern Mexico. They are simple to make, and I always find my family asking for more.

12 corn tortillas, warmed on a comal or frying pan

1 pound carne asada (recipe page 75)

1 cup chopped green cabbage

½ white onion, minced

½ bunch cilantro, finely chopped

6 wedges of key lime

6 chiles tepinas

Place two tortillas, one on top of the other, on each plate. Place 3 tablespoons of carne asada in the center of each tortilla. Top with cabbage, onion, and cilantro. Set 1 lime wedge and 1 chile tepín on the side of each plate.

Serve with grilled spring onions and whole red radishes, salted, with a squeeze of key lime juice on top.

SERVES 6

OPPOSITE: *Taco de Carne Asada (recipe above), and Salsa de la Casa (recipe page 66).*

TACOS DE POLLO

CHICKEN TACOS

If you like chicken tacos at your local Mexican restaurant, try these. They're easy, crunchy, and sure to please.

1 pound pollo deshebrado (recipe page 70)

12 corn tortillas, warmed on a comal or frying pan

Corn oil for frying

Shredded lettuce

½ pound queso Ranchero, crumbled

Salsa Ranchera (recipe page 67)

GRINGO APPROVED

Place 2 to 3 tablespoons of pollo deshebrado in each tortilla and fold closed. Using tongs to hold the tortilla closed, fry each taco in the oil until crisp. Place on a paper towel to drain; salt immediately. Top each taco with lettuce and a little queso Ranchero. Serve with Salsa Ranchera.

SERVES 6

TACOS DE CAMARONES

SHRIMP TACOS

This is an upscale version of the shrimp taco. With the Camarones en Mojo de Ajo, they are fine dining and a great taco all rolled up in one flavorful dish.

12 corn tortillas, warmed on a comal or frying pan
1 pound Camarones en Mojo de Ajo (recipe page 108)
½ white onion, minced
½ bunch cilantro, finely chopped
6 key lime wedges
6 chiles tepinas
Salsa para Mariscos (recipe page 55)

GRINGO
BEWARE

Place two tortillas, one on top of the other, on each plate. Place 2 or 3 pieces of shrimp in the center of each tortilla. Top with onion and cilantro, and set 1 lime wedge and 1 chile tepín on the side of each dish. Serve with Salsa para Mariscos.

SERVES 6

Tacos de Pescado al estilo Norte del Baja

NORTH BAJA–STYLE FISH TACOS

Down in Mexico, and especially in Baja, they serve just about any breaded fish in tacos. Try this recipe with shrimp, scallops, oysters, or whatever you like.

1 egg	Corn oil for deep frying
¼ cup milk	Salt to taste
¼ cup water	24 corn tortillas
¼ cup flour	½ head green cabbage, shredded
½ teaspoon salt	1 bunch cilantro, cleaned and finely chopped
½ teaspoon baking powder	1 white onion, finely chopped
¼ teaspoon dry mustard	5 key limes cut into wedges
2 pounds red snapper fillets	12 chiles tepinas
	Salsa para Mariscos (recipe page 55)

MODERATE

GRINGO APPROVED

Beat the egg with the milk and water. Add flour, salt, baking powder, and mustard, and beat until smooth. Cut fish into pieces 2½ to 3 inches long and 1 inch wide. Dip fish into batter until well-coated.

Heat oil to 375 degrees. Deep fry until golden brown and crisp. As soon as fish is cooked, drain on paper towels and salt lightly.

While fish is deep frying, heat the tortillas, one at a time, on comal until soft and pliable. Place one piece of fish on a hot tortilla. Top with shredded cabbage, cilantro, and white onion. Serve each with a wedge of lime, a chile tepín and Salsa para Mariscos.

SERVES 12

FLAUTAS

FLUTES

Flautas are rolled tacos that are fried. They are nothing like those little rock-hard taquitos you find in the frozen-food section of your local grocer. This recipe works well with several different fillings.

Corn oil for frying

2 dozen 6-inch corn tortillas

1 pound pollo deshebrado, ropa vieja, or carnitas (recipes pages 70, 76, 77)

½ white onion, chopped

2 tablespoons chopped cilantro

½ cup shredded potatoes (I use frozen hash-brown potatoes, thawed)

Salsa de Tomatillo y Aguacate (recipe page 56)

Heat the oil in a large, deep skillet to 375 degrees. Dip each tortilla in the oil for a few seconds, but not until crisp. Set the tortillas on a plate covered with a dish towel.

Mix the meat, onion, cilantro, and potato together. (The potato causes the mixture to bind.) Place about 3 tablespoons of the mixture in the center of each tortilla and roll up. Use a toothpick to hold the flauta closed. Deep fry the flautas, 2 or 3 at a time, until golden brown. Remove from oil and drain on paper towels. Salt and serve immediately with Salsa de Tomatillo y Aguacate.

SERVES 10

TAMALES DE PUERCO

PORK TAMALES

This is the tamale we eat every Christmas. They say if you get an olive you're very lucky, so I always put one olive in each tamale.

FILLING

2 pounds carnitas (recipe page 77)

1 (14½-ounce) can hominy

24 Spanish olives

MODERATE

GRINGO
APPROVED

Follow basic tamale instructions below. To fill, use 1 tablespoon carnitas, 1 teaspoon of hominy, and then 1 Spanish olive for filling. Steam for 1 hour. Serve with warm Salsa Colorada (recipe page 59).

MAKES 24 TAMALES

MAKING TAMALES

1. Soak corn husks in warm water overnight. Make masa in a blender following the instructions on the package. I use about ⅛ less lard than called for.

2. Spread 1 to 2 tablespoons of prepared masa onto a corn husk and add 1 tablespoon filling.

3. Roll up the tamale and tie the ends with strips of corn husk.

4. It is very important to arrange the tamales standing up on their ends in the steamer to ensure even cooking. Steaming time varies from one type of tamale to another. Serve with a warm sauce.

TAMALES VERDES DE MAÍZ TIERNO

GREEN CORN TAMALES

Green corn tamales are my mother-in-law's favorite. They have an unexpected green chile flavor in the background. I just have one thing to say about them… Yummmm!

6 ears sweet corn

½ cup milk

½ cup lard

¼ cup sweet butter

2 teaspoons salt

1 teaspoon sugar

1 cup queso Oaxaca, grated

2 roasted poblano chiles, seeded, peeled, and cut into strips

Cut the corn off the husks and coarsely grind in a food processor. Add the milk, lard, butter, and salt, and process to a smooth paste. Stir cheese into mixture.

Follow basic tamale recipe on page 91. To fill, use 1 tablespoon corn mixture and top with a strip of poblano chile. Roll and tie. Steam for 45 minutes and serve topped with Salsa de Tomatillo Verde (recipe page 64).

MAKES 24 TAMALES

PICTURED ON PAGE 90: *Tamales de Puerco (recipe page 91), and Salsa Colorada para Enchiladas (recipe page 59).*

This is where American-style Mexican food gets really ugly. The worst, by far, has to be the convenience-store microwave burrito. First of all, what is that filling made from? It sort of looks like some kind of meat substance with a gelatinous spicy gravy, but I've never met anyone who knows for sure. And those tortillas! I swear they're part Elmer's glue, they're so gummy and sticky.

BURRITOS, ENCHILADAS, AND QUESADILLAS

BURRITOS, ENCHILADAS, *y* QUESADILLAS

So you run in, pop one in the microwave, and two and a half minutes later you hear "Ding!" It's time to check out with your half-cooked burrito and the seventy-four ounce soda pop. Have you ever noticed the guy behind the counter glance over at the Tums when you're buying one of these belly bombs?

Miles down the road, you discover that the microwave didn't heat your burrito evenly. One bite burns your mouth and the next is like a frozen burrito-sicle. So you choke it down anyway or toss it out the window (better not—if a stray dog or cat gets a hold of it, it could be considered cruelty to animals).

On the other hand, the burritos, enchiladas, and quesadillas down in Mexico are delicious home cooking at its very best. Authentic quesadillas are light, turnover-like pastries filled with cheese and meat or vegetables. Enchiladas are topped with a crumbly white cheese and any one of a dozen or so homemade chile-based sauces, creating an array of flavors unknown to the average gringo. Burritos are made with hot, fresh, handmade tortillas that are so light, if you don't put a brick on top of them, they might float away. The fillings include roasted meats, homemade green chile, delicious beans, and vegetables. Best of all, the recipes are so easy that anyone can make them.

BURRITOS DE HUEVOS CON MACHACA

EGG AND MACHACA BURRITOS

If you like machaca and eggs, these breakfast burritos are quick and easy to make when you're on the run.

2 large flour tortillas, warmed on a comal or frying pan

Double batch of Huevos con Machaca (recipe page 16)

2 tablespoons queso Oaxaca, grated

Salsa de la Casa (recipe page 66)

MODERATE

GRINGO
APPROVED

Lay a tortilla on a flat, clean surface. Pour one batch of Huevos con Machaca in a line down the center of the tortilla, keeping back from the edges a few inches. Sprinkle with queso Oaxaca and Salsa de la Casa. Fold bottom up and then the sides in one at a time (see instructions on page 95). Serve warm.

MAKES 2 BURRITOS

BURRITOS DE FRIJOLES

BEAN BURRITOS

If you've got a bunch of kids around, think of these sort of like Mexican hot dogs. Make up a big plate of them. They're easy, and the kids will snack on them all day.

12 large flour tortillas, warmed on a comal or frying pan
9 cups Frijoles Refritos (recipe page 28), warm
½ white onion, finely chopped
1½ cups queso Oaxaca, grated

Lay a tortilla on a flat, clean surface. Pour ¾ of a cup of beans in a line down the center of the tortilla, keeping back from the edges a few inches. Sprinkle with onion and cheese. Fold bottom up and then the sides in one at a time (see instructions below). Serve warm.

GRINGO
FRIENDLY

MAKES 12 BURRITOS

MAKING BURRITOS

1. First, form the filling in a line down the center of a warmed flour tortilla, keeping back from the edges an inch or two. Don't overfill the burrito like they do in the gringo joints.

2. Fold the bottom up. . . .

3. Then fold one side over and roll it up.

4. See? This is easy.

BURRITOS DE CHILE VERDE

GREEN CHILE BURRITOS

When made correctly, there is simply nothing better than a good green chile burrito. Add an ice-cold Mexican beer, and it's a delicious, little Mexican vacation.

6 large flour tortillas, warmed on a comal or frying pan

4½ cups Chile Verde (recipe page 71), warm

½ white onion, finely chopped

½ cup finely chopped cilantro

Lay a tortilla on a flat, clean surface. Pour ¾ of a cup of Chile Verde in a line down the center of the tortilla, keeping back from the edges a few inches. Sprinkle with onion and cilantro. Fold bottom up and then the sides in one at a time (see instructions on page 95). Serve warm.

MAKES 6 BURRITOS

BURRITOS DE CHILE COLORADO

RED CHILE BURRITOS

If you like the red chile from northern Mexico, you'll love these burritos. They're mildly spicy and very delicious.

6 large flour tortillas, warmed on a comal or frying pan
4½ cups Chile Colorado (recipe page 72), warm
½ white onion, finely chopped

GRINGO
APPROVED

Lay a tortilla on a flat, clean surface. Pour ¾ of a cup of Chile Colorado in a line down the center of the tortilla, keeping back from the edges a few inches. Sprinkle with onion. Fold bottom up and then the sides in one at a time (see instructions on page 95). Serve warm.

MAKES 6 BURRITOS

ENCHILADAS DE POLLO

CHICKEN ENCHILADAS

Homemade chicken enchiladas are the mark of a good Mexican cook. So cook up a few of these burritos and show your talents as a Mexican chef.

1½ cups pollo deshebrado (recipe page 70)

½ cup chopped white onion

¼ cup chopped cilantro

12 corn tortillas lightly fried in corn oil, still warm

2½ cups Salsa de Tomatillo Verde (recipe page 64), warm

½ cup queso Cotija, crumbled

MODERATE

GRINGO APPROVED

Mix the chicken, onion, and cilantro together. Dip the tortillas, one at a time, into the Salsa de Tomatillo Verde and then place about 3 or 4 tablespoons of the chicken mixture in the center of the tortilla and roll up. Place in a baking dish.

After all the enchiladas are in the baking dish, pour remaining sauce over the enchiladas and place under the broiler for a few minutes to warm. You may also do this with individual plates. Remove from broiler. Place two enchiladas on each plate and top with 1 tablespoon queso Cotija. Serve immediately.

SERVES 6

OPPOSITE: *Enchiladas de Pollo (recipe above), Salsa de Tomatillo Verde (recipe page 64), and Arroz a la Mexicana (recipe page 30).*

ENCHILADAS DE CARNE

BEEF ENCHILADAS

The beef enchilada you find in a typical U.S. Mexican restaurant is one of my biggest pet peeves. Why would anybody in their right mind use ground beef in their enchiladas? This recipe takes enchiladas to the next level.

12 corn tortillas lightly fried in corn oil, still warm
2½ cups Salsa Colorada (recipe page 59), warm
2 cups machaca (recipe page 74)
½ cup queso Cotija, crumbled

Dip the tortillas, one at a time, into the Salsa Colorada and then place about 3 or 4 tablespoons of the Machaca in the center of the tortilla and roll up. Place in a baking dish.

After all the enchiladas are in the baking dish, pour remaining sauce over the enchiladas and place under the broiler for a few minutes to warm. You may also do this with individual plates. Remove from broiler. Place two enchiladas on each plate and top with 1 tablespoon queso Cotija. Serve immediately.

SERVES 6

ENCHILADAS DE QUESO

CHEESE ENCHILADAS

This is your basic authentic cheese enchilada. If you've never been to Mexico, "Hold onto your sombrero," because it's nothing like the enchiladas that come with that #4 combination plate down at "Billy's Ranchero."

1 ½ cups queso Cotija, crumbled

¾ cup chopped white onion

12 corn tortillas lightly fried in corn oil

2 ½ cups Salsa Colorada (recipe page 59), warm

Mix about ¾ of the cheese and onion together. Dip the tortillas, one at a time, into the Salsa Colorada and then place about 3 or 4 tablespoons of the cheese mixture in the center of the tortilla and roll up. Place in a baking dish.

After all the enchiladas are in the baking dish, pour remaining sauce over the enchiladas and place under the broiler for a few minutes to warm and melt the cheese. You may also do this with individual plates. Remove from broiler. Place two enchiladas on each plate and top with about 1 tablespoon queso Cotija. Serve immediately.

SERVES 6

QUESADILLAS MEXICANA

MEXICAN QUESADILLAS

Quesadillas in Mexico are different from the cheese crisps served in the Mexican restaurants in the U.S. They are more like little turnovers filled with a good, melting cheese.

1 pound premixed tortilla masa

2 cups shredded queso Oaxaca or your favorite melting cheese

Corn oil for frying, heated up to 375 degrees

Salt to taste

GRINGO
FRIENDLY

Roll the dough into 16 little balls. Then, one at a time, place the dough balls into a tortilla press between two sheets of plastic (I use plastic kitchen bags) and form a 3 ½- to 4-inch tortilla. Remove the top sheet of plastic and pick up the tortilla along with the bottom sheet of plastic. Place the tortilla, plastic side down, in the palm of your hand. Place 2 tablespoons of queso Oaxaca in the center of each tortilla. Using the plastic, fold the tortilla over and gently press the edges together to form a seal. Remove plastic and fry in hot oil until golden brown, one or two at a time. Drain thoroughly on paper towels, salt to taste, and serve hot.

MAKES 16

QUESADILLA DE PAPAS Y CHORIZO

POTATO AND CHORIZO QUESADILLAS

This is a great little snack when you have a crowd. It's like Mexico's version of a calozone—easy to make, flavorful, and pleasing to everyone.

½ pound chorizo
½ pound white potatoes, unpeeled, cut into ½-inch cubes
2 canned chipotle chiles
1 teaspoon of the adobo sauce from the can

GRINGO
BEWARE

Fry the chorizo until cooked but not browned; drain all but 2 tablespoons of the grease from the chorizo. Add the potatoes, chiles, and sauce, and continue cooking until potatoes are soft and starting to brown. Remove from heat.

Follow the quesadilla recipe on page 102, except use only 1 tablespoon of cheese filling and add 1 tablespoon of the chorizo filling.

MAKES 12 TO 15 QUESADILLAS

QUESADILLA DE FLOR DE CALABAZA

SQUASH FLOWER QUESADILLAS

This authentic Mexican treat will blow the minds of your friends and family. Just ask your grocer to order the squash flowers for you.

7 cups squash blossoms

2 tablespoons corn oil

½ white onion, finely chopped

2 cloves garlic, minced

1 poblano chile, roasted and peeled, roughly chopped

1 teaspoon salt

MODERATE

GRINGO APPROVED

Clean and remove the pistils and stems from the squash flowers and roughly chop. Sauté the onion and garlic in the oil until translucent. Add the poblano chile and sauté for 1 minute. Add the squash flowers and salt, and cover for 10 minutes, stirring a few times. Remove lid and cook off any excess liquid so that the filling is just moist.

Follow the quesadilla recipe on page 102, except use only 1 tablespoon of cheese filling and add 1 tablespoon of the squash filling.

MAKES 24 QUESADILLAS

104

When I was ten years old, I went on my first Mexican fishing trip to the village at Kino Bay. We headed out to Isla Tiburón (Shark Island). All the men put a dollar into the pool, betting on who would catch the biggest fish. The fish weren't biting, so our Mexican guide decided it was time to go around the island. I tried to pull up my line, but it seemed to be caught on the bottom. The guide helped me free it, but I still had difficulty pulling it into the boat. To my surprise, I had a huge fish. The guide said in broken English, "Mexican Salmon." When we cleaned it, the meat was bright pink! For supper that night our guide grilled the fish over a mesquite fire and served it with fresh, hot tortillas, homemade rice, and a salsa that I think is still burning my mouth. And, with my dinner, I was given all the dollars from the betting pool.

The waters surrounding Mexico are teaming with fish and shellfish. Fishing and shrimping are major industries, so extremely fresh fish and shellfish are readily available and reasonably inexpensive to the average family in Mexico. Combine this with the fact that Mexico is predominantly a Catholic nation (you remember the old tradition of fish on Friday, and still today, fish during Lent), and what you get are several million Mexican people eating muchos pescados y mariscos.

FISH AND SHELLFISH
PESCADOS *y* MARISCOS

Eating fish is ingrained in the culture, and the recipes in this chapter offer a glimpse of just how delicious and diverse they can be. If your idea of Mexican food is mostly tacos, rice, and beans, you are in for a real treat. I'd start with Camarones Mojo de Ajo, which means shrimp wet with garlic. It's a spicy, mouth-watering Mexican version of the best scampi you've ever eaten. These are some of my favorite seafood recipes, and I just know they'll be your favorites, too! So buy some fish and invite some friends and family over. Light the grill and crack open a few ice cold cervezas. Life is good!

Gulf of California

MEXICO

Gulf of Mexico

Pacific Ocean

CALLO DE HACHA CON AGUACATE

SCALLOP-STUFFED AVOCADOS

Forget about chips and salsa and try this great summertime appetizer. It is light and spicy, full of flavor, and reminicent of a day in the sun on a Mexican beach.

⅓ cup freshly squeezed key lime juice

1 tablespoon fresh cilantro, finely chopped

1 teaspoon Mexican oregano

⅓ cup extra-virgin olive oil

¾ pound bay scallops

Salt to taste

Freshly ground black pepper to taste

3 ripe Haas avocados

1 serrano chile, julienned

MODERATE

GRINGO
APPROVED

In a medium glass mixing bowl, whisk together the lime juice, cilantro, and oregano, then continue whisking while drizzling in the olive oil. Add the scallops and season with salt and pepper. Stir well, cover, and refrigerate for 30 minutes.

Meanwhile, cut the avocados in half and remove the seeds. Scoop out about half of the avocado with a melon baller, making little balls of avocado and leaving a good amount of avocado around the sides of the shell. After the scallops have marinated for 30 minutes, carefully stir in the balls of avocado. Scoop out the scallop mixture with a slotted spoon and stuff each avocado half. Top with shreds of serrano chile.

SERVES 6

COCKTAIL DE CAMARONES

SHRIMP COCKTAIL

I love sitting on a Mexican beach with an ice-cold beer, watching the fishing boats come and go while enjoying one of these delicious little wonders.

¼ cup V-8 Juice

(I know what you're thinking—yes, they have V-8 juice in Mexico!)

¼ cup catsup

¼ cup freshly squeezed key lime juice

2 teaspoons Tapatio sauce (or your favorite bottled Mexican hot sauce)

1 pound boiled medium shrimp, peeled and deveined

½ cup chopped fresh plum tomato

¼ cup chopped white onion

¼ cup seeded and chopped cucumber

¼ cup fresh cilantro, finely chopped

1 serrano chile, seeds removed and minced

2 avocados

MODERATE

GRINGO
APPROVED

Mix together the V-8 Juice, catsup, lime juice, and hot sauce. Add shrimp, tomato, onion, cucumber, cilantro, and chile; stir well. Cover and chill for 3 hours. Prior to serving, cut the avocados into ½-inch cubes and gently fold into the shrimp; serve in margarita glasses.

SERVES 4

CAMARONES EN MOJO DE AJO

SHRIMP IN GARLIC SAUCE

If you love shrimp, you have to try this recipe. The garlic, chiles, butter, and shrimp make this dish delicious. It's Mexico's version of scampi.

5 cloves garlic

1 teaspoon coarse salt

5 black peppercorns

2 chiles de arboles

3 tablespoons butter

1 pound medium shrimp, peeled

In a molcajete, crush and grind the garlic and salt to a paste. Then grind in the black peppercorns and chiles de arboles. Set aside.

In a medium sauté pan, melt the butter until it is bubbling but not browned; add the shrimp. Sauté until almost done, then add the garlic mixture. Continue cooking until the shrimp are done and the garlic has fully cooked.

SERVES 4

OPPOSITE: *Camarones en Mojo de Ajo (recipe above).*

CHILES RELLENOS CON CAMARONES

SHRIMP-STUFFED POBLANO CHILES

Relleno means "stuffed." This recipe is not, as many people will think, for a batter-dipped, deep fried chile stuffed with cheese. However, it is very authentic and so delicious.

8 poblano chiles, roasted, seeded, and peeled

1 pound small shrimp, cooked and peeled

2 celery hearts, finely chopped

2 medium-size red potatoes, boiled until tender, peeled and cut into small cubes

2 tablespoons Italian parsley, finely chopped

¾ cup heavy mayonnaise

Salt and pepper to taste

DRESSING

⅓ cup olive oil

2 cloves garlic, finely chopped

1 large white onion, thinly sliced

2 medium carrots, washed, peeled, and cut into rounds

⅓ cup white wine vinegar

¼ cup water

1 sprig fresh thyme

1 sprig fresh marjoram

1 teaspoon whole black peppercorns

1 whole clove

1 bay leaf

MODERATE

GRINGO APPROVED

Sauté the garlic, onion, and carrots in the oil over medium heat until the onion is translucent. Add remaining dressing ingredients; bring to a boil for 3 minutes. Remove from heat and add the poblano chiles. Marinate the chiles in the dressing for 3 hours.

Remove and drain the chiles, saving the dressing. Toss together the shrimp, celery, potatoes, parsley, mayonnaise, salt, and pepper. Stuff the chiles with the shrimp mixture and arrange on a platter. Pour the dressing over the stuffed chiles and serve.

SERVES 8

CAMARONES ENDIABLADOS

DEVILED SHRIMP

The use of toasted chiles in this dish adds a richness to these delicious, deviled shrimp. Now, this is real Mexican eating!

2 ancho chiles, stem, seeds, and veins removed

1 negro chile, stem, seeds, and veins removed

3 plum tomatoes

1 clove garlic, whole, plus four cloves, minced

3 tablespoons butter

3 tablespoons corn oil

½ white onion, thinly sliced lengthwise

1 pound medium shrimp, peeled and deveined

1 tablespoon Worcestershire sauce

2 tablespoons consomé de pollo (recipe page 45) or chicken broth

¼ cup dry white wine

Salt and pepper to taste

Toast the chiles on a comal until soft and pliable. Simmer them in enough water to cover for 15 minutes. Drain the chiles and purée them in a blender with the tomatoes and whole garlic clove. Work the blender mixture through a wire sieve into a glass bowl with the back of a spoon until only the chile solids are left. Discard solids and set bowl aside.

In a large skillet, heat the butter and oil, and sauté the onion and minced garlic until the onion is translucent. Add the shrimp and cook until they start to change color. Add chile sauce, Worcestershire sauce, and consomé; stir, cover, and simmer for two minutes, then add the white wine and allow to simmer a few minutes more. Season to taste and serve.

SERVES 4

CAZUELA DE ALMEJAS

CLAM CASSEROLE

Try out this fun way to cook. A cazuela is an earthenware pan or pot from Mexico. You can also do this in a heavy frying pan.

2 pounds large Mexican or cherrystone clams

1 tablespoon corn oil

4 cloves garlic, chopped

½ white onion, chopped

2 tablespoons Italian parsley, finely chopped

1 cup dry white wine

Juice of 2 key limes

½ cup water

2 tablespoons breadcrumbs

GRINGO
FRIENDLY

Wash the clams very well with a brush to remove sand. Place them in a bowl of salted water. Slowly raise the heat under the cazuela to medium. (If you heat it too rapidly, it will crack. And never put a cold cazuela or earthenware dish of any kind directly over a flame or a hot burner.)

Add the oil and fry the garlic and onion until soft, then remove the clams from the salted water and add them to the cazuela, turning them until they open. Discard any clams that do not open. Add the parsley, wine, lime juice, and water. Bring to a simmer. Sprinkle with the breadcrumbs and let it simmer for 5 minutes more. Salt to taste and then use the cazuela for serving at the table.

SERVES 4

OPPOSITE: *Cazuela de Almejas (recipe above).*

113

CEVICHE

CONCH MARINATED IN CITRUS

The average gringo will look at this recipe and say, "Wait a minute. When do you cook the fish?"
By marinating the conch in the citrus juices, it will be cured rather than cooked. Give it a try!

1¼ pounds conch

⅓ cup freshly squeezed lemon juice

3 tablespoons freshly squeezed key lime juice

3 tablespoons freshly squeezed orange juice

2 teaspoons freshly grated ginger

1 serrano chile, minced

Zest of 1 lime

½ bunch cilantro, finely chopped

½ cup chopped green onion

½ cup finely diced red bell pepper

2 cloves garlic, minced

3 tablespoons extra-virgin olive oil

DRESSING

1 large ripe Haas avocado, chopped

1 Roma tomato, peeled, seeded, and finely chopped

1 tablespoon finely chopped cilantro

1 tablespoon finely chopped white onion

1 jalapeño chile, seeded and minced

1 clove garlic, minced

Juice of 1 key lime

Pinch of dark brown sugar

1½ tablespoons extra-virgin olive oil

Salt and freshly ground black pepper to taste

Fresh key lime wedges for garnish

Rinse the conch under very cold water and dry with a paper towel. Cut the conch into ½-inch chunks. In a large, non-reactive bowl, mix together the lemon juice, lime juice, orange juice, ginger, serrano chile, and lime zest. Mix well, then add the conch. Gently stir, cover, and refrigerate for 1 hour or until the conch turns white. Add the cilantro, green onion, red bell pepper, two cloves garlic, and olive oil. Cover and refrigerate for 2 to 3 hours.

Gently fold all dressing ingredients together and then season to taste. Using a slotted spoon, divide the ceviche between six plates. Spoon the dressing over the ceviche and then drizzle on a little of the ceviche marinade. Serve with ice-cold Mexican beer and wedges of fresh key limes.

SERVES 6

HUACHINANGO A LA PARILLA

GRILLED RED SNAPPER

Here's one from the beaches around Acapulco. Due to the fact that red snapper is so plentiful in coastal waters, it's the most popular fish in Mexico.

1 (5-pound) red snapper, butterflied

MARINADE

¼ cup heavy mayonnaise

Juice of 3 key limes

2 teaspoons salt

½ teaspoon freshly ground black pepper

FOR BASTING

1 stick melted butter

1 clove garlic, minced

CHILE SAUCE

8 guajillo chiles, seeds and veins removed

6 ancho chiles, seeds and veins removed

5 plum tomatoes, skinned and seeded

4 cloves garlic

1 tablespoon white vinegar

3 whole cloves

¼ white onion

¼ teaspoon ground cumin

½ teaspoon ground thyme

½ teaspoon marjoram

½ teaspoon Mexican oregano

1 cup water

2 tablespoons corn oil

2 tablespoons butter

Salt and pepper to taste

Rinse fish under cold water and then pat dry with a paper towel. Combine marinade ingredients in a non-reactive bowl. Rub fish inside with marinade and then place in bowl with marinade. Cover and place in a cool spot, but not in the refrigerator, for ½ hour.

Place the chiles in a bowl and cover with boiling water. Let stand for 15 minutes and then drain. Purée the chiles in a blender until smooth along with the tomatoes, garlic, vinegar, cloves, onion, spices, and 1 cup of water. In a saucepan, heat the oil and butter. Add the chile purée and simmer until sauce thickens, stirring often. Add salt and pepper to taste. Allow sauce to cool.

Place the fish on a lightly greased grill, about 8 inches above hot mesquite charcoal, skin side down. Cook for about 15 minutes. Baste the flesh side with the chile sauce 3 to 5 times. Mix the melted butter and 2 cloves garlic together.

Carefully flip the fish using a large steak spatula. Baste the scale side with the melted garlic butter occasionally while grilling for 10 minutes, or until fish is fully cooked.

SERVES 6

HUACHINANGO A LA VERACRUZANO

VERACRUZ RED SNAPPER

This famous dish is very popular on both sides of the border. If you're just learning to cook, this is a great place to start.

1 (4½-pound) red snapper

Salt and pepper to taste

5 medium plum tomatoes, sliced

½ cup pimento-stuffed olives

2 tablespoons capers, rinsed

1 tablespoon Mexican oregano

3 bay leaves

3 sprigs fresh thyme

4 garlic cloves, peeled and thinly sliced

2 white onions, thinly sliced

8 güero chiles, whole

½ cup extra-virgin olive oil

GRINGO BEWARE

Preheat oven to 375 degrees.

Rinse the fish under very cold water, then dry with a paper towel. Sprinkle with salt and pepper and place in a large baking dish. Top with all ingredients except olive oil, then drizzle with olive oil. Bake for 45 minutes or until the fish is fully cooked, basting the fish several times during baking.

SERVES 6

OPPOSITE: *Huachinango a la Veracruzano (recipe above).*

SWEETS *and* DESSERTS
DULCES *y*

Whenever you go to a foreign country, you quickly find out that the rest of the world doesn't hold the same opinions that we take for granted as fact. Take the case of sugar. Here, we eat sugar but we try to avoid it. In Mexico, they eat sugar every day, and I mean a lot of it. It's like the U.S. in the fifties. They eat sugary pastries in the morning with coffee, for lunch it's soda pop with twice as much sugar as the stuff you find here in the U.S., and for the main meal of the day, dessert and possibly a little sweet pastry with coffee later. Diet soda and light beer are hard to find outside of the resorts. This is because Mexicans are less hung up on the issues of diet and body shape. When I first got to know some Mexican people as friends, I found they would call me "gordo" (fat). I was offended, but later I came to realize that this was not an insult but rather a description, like tall or fair-skinned, and that they would never knowingly do anything to hurt my feelings. In short, they worry less and try to enjoy life a lot more, and their desserts and sweets are no exception to this.

POSTRES

In this chapter, you'll find some of my favorite recipes for traditional Mexican pastries and sweets. Try the Pastel de Tres Leches. It's a delicious white cake with a light, whipped-cream frosting that weeps a little sweet, cold cream into every bite. These recipes are the perfect ending to a night of great Mexican dining.

BUÑUELOS DEL NORTE

FRITTERS FROM NORTHERN MEXICO

If you like sopapias, try these fritters—they're much better. They make a fun treat when served with vanilla ice cream, and the kids will love them!

1 cup all-purpose flour

¾ teaspoon baking powder

1 teaspoon granulated sugar

¼ teaspoon salt

⅓ cup milk

1 large egg

Canola oil for frying

¼ cup powdered sugar

1 cup piloncillo or brown sugar

1 cup water

1 canela or cinnamon stick

In a small sauce pan dissolve the brown sugar in the water, add the cinnamon stick and bring to a boil over medium heat, reduce until thick.

Mix together the flour, baking powder, sugar, and salt. In a second mixing bowl, lightly beat the milk and egg, and then stir it into the flour mixture until fully mixed but do not over mix. Cover and allow to rest for 15 minutes. Meanwhile, dissolve the piloncillo in the hot water, add canela stick, and bring to a low boil in a sauce-pan over medium heat and reduce until thick. Set aside.

Heat about 3 inches of oil to 375° in a Dutch oven or deep frying pan. Drop 2 spoonfuls of batter in the oil at a time and fry, turning a few times, until golden brown. Dust with powdered sugar and serve piloncillo syrup on the side for dipping.

MAKES 8 SERVINGS

PLÁTANOS EN ROMPOPE

BANANAS IN EGGNOG

This is a great traditional Mexican dessert to serve to adults after a night of dining due to the fact that it is not overly sweet.

4 ripe bananas, still a little firm
2 cups warm Rompope (recipe page 133)
¼ cup sliced almonds

Peel the bananas. Using your thumb, press into the seam of the banana and then follow the seam lengthwise (the banana will split into thirds). Place the three sections into a serving dish or on a salad plate. Repeat with all three bananas.

Drizzle about ½ cup warm Rompope over each plate of bananas and then sprinkle with 1 tablespoon sliced almonds. Serve immediately.

SERVES 4

PICO DE GALLO

BEAK OF THE ROOSTER

Pico de Gallo is a different dish in different parts of Mexico. In Juarez, it is a salsa as fiery as the stinging bite of a pecking rooster. This refreshing fruit salad from Sonora, Mexico, is served on hot days and is eaten by picking at the bowl with your thumb and forefinger, resembling the rooster's beak.

4 cups ripe, assorted melons, cut into 1-inch cubes

1 pineapple, trimmed, center removed, cut into 1-inch cubes (a 14-ounce can of diced pineapple will do)

½ jicama, cut into ½-inch cubes

1 cucumber, peeled and seeded, cut into ½-inch cubes

Juice of 4 key limes

6 chiles tepinas

GRINGO
BEWARE

Mix all ingredients in a bowl except limes and chiles. Let stand, covered, in refrigerator for one hour. Spoon fruit into cups, giving each a little of the juice from the bowl. Top each with lime juice and a crushed chile tepín or a light sprinkle of cayenne pepper. Serve immediately.

SERVES 6

FLAN

FLAN

This delicious custard is by far Mexico's most famous dessert. It is a perfect way to complete an elegant Mexican meal.

¾ cup plus 2 tablespoons sugar

2 cups milk

2 eggs plus 1 yolk, lightly beaten

Pinch of salt

½ teaspoon vanilla extract

GARNISH

Fresh sliced strawberries, orange zest, slivered almonds, Kahlua

Preheat oven to 350 degrees.

Place ¾ cup sugar in a skillet over medium-high heat. Be careful, as this an easy place to get burned. Stir the sugar constantly while it melts and turns medium brown. Remove from heat, pour to coat bottom of four 6-ounce ramekins. Allow to cool slightly.

Scald the milk in a double boiler. Whisk together the eggs, 2 tablespoons sugar, salt, and vanilla extract. Slowly whisk into the hot milk. Pour through a strainer into a bowl and spoon into the ramekins until almost full. Place a large pot, with lid, in the oven. Place the ramekins in the pot and add 1 inch of water, creating a water bath (be careful not to pour any water into the ramekins).

Cover and bake for 20 to 25 minutes or until a knife inserted in the center of the flan comes out clean. Top with sliced strawberries, orange zest, and a few slivered almonds, then drizzle with a little Kahlua.

SERVES 4

PAN DE MUERTOS

BREAD OF THE DEAD

These sweet little breads are served on El Día de los Muertos, The Day of the Dead. This day is celebrated throughout Mexico and in most Mexican American communities. Traditionally, it is believed that the souls of the dead return to visit their families on this day. This is a warm-hearted day of rememberance, a time to honor family and friends who have died.

2 packages active dry yeast	1 tablespoon shortening
5 tablespoons warm milk	2 teaspoons ground cinnamon
7½ cups all-purpose flour, sifted	2 teaspoons pure vanilla extract
2 cups sugar	½ cup milk
1 cup plus 2 tablespoons butter	Sugar for dusting
12 eggs	

Dissolve the yeast in the warm milk; stir, cover, and let stand for 10 minutes. Make a mound out of the flour in a mixing bowl and create a well in the center. Place the sugar, butter, yeast, eggs, shortening, cinnamon, vanilla, and milk in the well. Work the mixture into a dough and knead until the dough pulls away from the sides of the mixing bowl. If the dough is too soft, work in more flour. Shape the dough into a ball. Rub a little shortening on the outside, flour it lightly, and place in a clean, lightly greased mixing bowl and cover with plastic wrap. Let stand in a warm place for 2½ hours, or until doubled. Refrigerate overnight.

Pinch off and roll the dough into balls the size of an orange. Then make little strips of dough to look like bones and place on top of each bread. Place the rolls on greased baking sheets and let rise in a warm place until doubled in size (about 1½ hours).

Preheat oven to 350 degrees. Dust with sugar and bake for 30 minutes or until the bottoms sound hollow when tapped.

MAKES 6 TO 8 LOAVES

GALLETAS DE BODA

MEXICAN WEDDING COOKIES

These easy cookies are fantastic with coffee, and they're light enough to send a few along with a packed lunch. Everybody loves them, and by the way, you don't need to wait for a wedding to make up a batch (see photo on page 127).

1 cup butter, softened

½ cup powdered sugar, sifted, plus some to roll cookies in

1 teaspoon vanilla extract

2¼ cups all-purpose flour, sifted

½ teaspoon salt

¾ cup chopped walnuts

Combine the butter, powdered sugar, and vanilla in a mixing bowl and mix together well. Sift in the flour and salt, and then stir in the walnuts. Roll the dough into a ball and cover with plastic wrap, then place in the refrigerator to chill for 45 minutes.

Preheat oven to 400 degrees.

Roll the chilled dough into 1-inch balls. Bake on an ungreased baking sheet until just set but not browned. Allow the cookies to cool down enough to handle and roll in powdered sugar. Allow to cool fully and then roll in sugar again.

MAKES 4 DOZEN COOKIES

PASTEL DE TRES LECHES

THREE-MILK CAKE

This traditional Latin American cake is moist, almost to the point of being juicy. Top it off with whipped cream and strawberries, and as they say, "Now you're cooking!"

CAKE

1 tablespoon sweet butter, softened

5 eggs, separated

1 cup sugar

⅓ cup milk

1 teaspoon pure vanilla extract

1 cup all-purpose flour

2 teaspoons baking powder

MILK SYRUP

1 cup heavy whipping cream

1 (14-ounce) can condensed milk, sweetened

1 (12-ounce) can evaporated milk

2 tablespoons pure vanilla extract

GARNISH

Fresh strawberries, sliced

Whipped cream

Preheat oven to 350 degrees.

Butter a 13 x 9-inch baking dish. Beat egg yolks in medium-size bowl with ¾ cup of the sugar until the mixture is light in color (about five minutes). Carefully stir in milk, vanilla, flour, and baking powder, and set aside. Beat egg whites until peaks start to form. Add remaining sugar and continue beating until whites are stiff, but not dry. Carefully fold the egg whites into egg yolk mixture. Pour batter into baking dish and bake cake for about 45 minutes until a toothpick inserted in the middle of the cake comes out clean. Cool cake slightly before unmolding.

In a small saucepan, mix together heavy cream, condensed milk, and evaporated milk. Bring to a boil, stirring constantly. Add vanilla extract, remove from heat, and allow to cool slightly. Carefully pour milk syrup over cake a little at a time, spooning excess syrup back to the top of the cake until syrup is fully absorbed. Allow to fully cool down. Garnish with strawberries and whipped cream.

SERVES 10

OPPOSITE: *Pastel de Tres Leches (recipe above), and Galletas de Boda (recipe page 125).*

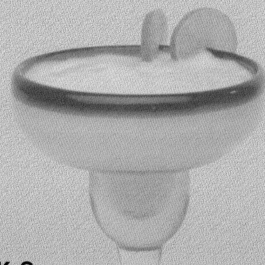

DRINKS

BEBIDAS

Around our house, if my wife wants to drink a cold beer she has one, but down in Mexico the story is a little different. Whenever you walk into a home in Mexico and a woman greets you, she will always offer you coffee or soda. If it's afternoon and you are greeted by a man, he will offer the men ice-cold beer and the ladies, once again, coffee or soda. This is the custom.

In Mexico, appearance is everything. Most women would never think of walking around drinking a beer at a dinner party; it would send the wrong message. There seems to be nothing wrong with her having a cocktail or glass of wine with dinner, but in Mexico, beer is much too crude for a lady. After spending some time in Mexico, I found that when some of the ladies wanted to sip on a cold one, their solution was a drink called "Burro Café" (Stubborn Coffee). They would go into the kitchen and pour beer into a dark coffee cup and have their beer while still keeping up appearances.

The drinks of Mexico are legendary and filled to the rim with romance. From their aromatic hot chocolate and thick, sweet coffee to tequila or homemade tepache, each drink helps to create that magical atmosphere you can always find down in Mexico. So the next time you're having a Mexican dinner party, be sure to try a few of these authentic drinks. And if you're serving beer, set out a few dark coffee cups for the ladies.

TEPACHE

PINEAPPLE COOLER

This is a homemade, pineapple-flavored, Mexican fiesta beverage with a kick! It's tropical, tart, and refreshing. Your guests will find it so amazing that it's homemade.

1 large, ripe pineapple	½ gallon water
2 canela sticks	1 pound dry barley
10 whole cloves	3 pounds piloncillo, broken up

Cut the top off the pineapple and discard. Wash the body of the pineapple and crush with a kitchen mallet, skin and all. Place in a large crock with canela and cloves and cover with ½ gallon of water. Cover crock with a kitchen towel or plastic wrap and let stand, unrefrigerated, for two days.

In a large saucepan, simmer the barley and piloncillo in 1 quart of water until the barley swells and cracks (about 1 hour). Allow the barley mixture to cool, then add to the crock with the pineapple mixture. Recover and let stand, unrefrigerated, for two more days. Strain well and serve over ice.

SERVES 10 TO 12

SANGRIA HELADA

ICED SANGRIA

Let's face it—on a hot summer day, everybody loves sangria! It is light, fruity, and so . . . refreshing!

¼ cup raw sugar	¼ cup Grand Marnier
½ cup orange juice	4 lemon slices
½ cup water	4 orange slices
1 bottle dry red wine	

In a saucepan, combine the sugar, orange juice, and water; simmer for 5 minutes while stirring. Remove from heat. Stir in wine, Grand Marnier, lemon, and orange slices. Pour into pitcher over ice. Find a shady spot and enjoy.

MAKES 6 TO 8 DRINKS

AGUA DE TAMARINDO

TAMARIND COOLER

This slightly sweet, tart, refreshing beverage is served throughout Mexico and Central America. It's just the thing on a hot day. Try it at your next pool party or barbecue. The kids will love it and so will you!

3 cups boiling water

½ pound tamarind pods, shells removed

⅔ cup sugar

Pour water over the tamarind and the sugar in a large mixing bowl. Allow to soak for 45 minutes, stirring often to dissolve the sugar and tamarind pulp. Strain through a sieve into a pitcher of ice and add water to fill. Discard seeds and tamarind pulp. Ahhh.

MAKES 8 CUPS

AGUA DE JAMAICA

JAMAICA FLOWER TEA

This refreshing drink is served all over Mexico. It's delicate, mildly sweet, and full of vitamin C. I think of it as Mexio's answer to Cool-Aid.

¾ cup honey

3 cups water

1 ½ cups dried Jamaica flowers*

Bring water and honey to a boil in a medium saucepan. Stir until the honey dissolves. Add the Jamaica flowers and steep for 15 minutes. Strain through a sieve into a pitcher of ice and add water to fill.

MAKES 8 CUPS

*Note: the direct translation of "Jamaica flower" is "Hibiscus flower," however, they are not the same. Certain varities of Hibiscus flowers are poisonous—do not use! Ask your local grocer or specialty food store for Jamaica flowers.

CAFÉ DE OLLA

COFFEE IN A CLAY POT

Try serving this Mexican coffee the next time friends stop by. It's okay if you don't have the clay pot, just serve it in big heavy mugs.

8 cups water

½ cup coarse, freshly ground coffee

1 canela stick

¼ cup sugar

Combine all ingredients in a large clay pot or saucepan and just bring to a boil, then turn heat to lowest setting and let steep for 20 minutes. Strain and serve.

SERVES 8

CHOCOLATE CALIENTE ESTILO MEXICANO

MEXICAN HOT CHOCOLATE

Legend has it that even Montezuma was addicted to this delicious beverage. You'll find your friends and family shouting for more!

4 cups milk

4 ounces Ibarra chocolate

1 teaspoon ground canela

In a medium saucepan over low heat, melt the chocolate into the milk, stirring constantly. Add the canela and whisk to a froth before serving hot.

SERVES 4

BÉSAME MUCHO

GIVE ME MANY KISSES

You may think that when coffee meets tequila, you will have something very aggresive on your hands—Not at all. This drink is elegant, and the perfect ending for that special Mexican meal!

1 cup strong coffee

¾ ounce your favorite dark tequila

¾ ounce damiana

Whipped cream

Orange zest for garnish

1 canela stick

Stir coffee, tequila, and damiana together. Pour into coffee mug; top with whipped cream and orange zest. Add canela stick for stirring.

MAKES 1 SERVING

ROMPOPE

MEXICAN EGGNOG

In Mexico, they love eggnog around the holidays just as much as we do. They love it so much that they usually make enough to give out to friends and family as Christmas gifts.

1 quart whole milk

1¼ cups sugar

1 vanilla bean, split lengthwise

10 eggs

1½ cups white rum

Bring the milk, sugar, and vanilla bean to a low boil in a medium saucepan. Reduce heat, cover, and simmer for 20 minutes. Remove from heat and allow to cool to room temperature. Remove vanilla bean and discard. Separate the eggs, discarding the whites (or freeze for future use). Beat the yolks well, then slowly whisk into the sweetened milk. Add the rum and stir well. Pour into glass bottles and refrigerate for 2 days before serving. May be served warm or cold or used as a dessert topping.

MAKES 2 QUARTS

TEQUILA

If your impression of tequila is that of a cheap, clear beverage mainly used by power-drinking college students on spring break trying to drink themselves into oblivion, you are not in the minority. However, you are missing what this extremely well-produced national treasure of Mexico is all about.

Here is a little test to check your level of gringoness: What is the #1 way that the people of Mexico drink tequila? If you said, "in margaritas," thank you for playing but no cigarro! I love a good margarita as much as the next guy, but truth be told, margaritas are for touristas. I was in Guadalajara as a guest of the Jose Cuervo Company doing research on tequila when I saw the light.

On page 137 is my recipe for Sangrita Mexicana. This is how the true aficionados of tequila drink it. A Sangrita Mexicana is served in two small brandy snifters about three inches tall, with tequila reposado in the first and in the second, a beverage called Sangrita, which is tomato-based and a little citrusy. You take a small sip of tequila and then a sip of Sangrita. This is often served with a shot glass of key lime juice or key lime juice mixed with Squirt Grapefruit Soda. This three-drink combination, being green, white, and red, is called a Bandera, or a Mexican Flag.

Tequila, like so many things from Mexico, is meant to be slowly savored, like a fine cognac. Chugging it down would simply be a waste of good tequila, not to mention the fact that you will get as drunk as a cow and everyone will know you're from out of town.

Another gringo misconception is that tequila is made from cactus. The agave is actually a member of the lily family and not a cactus at all. Tequila is only produced in Mexico, and by distilling the Agave Azul Tequilana Weber, also known as the blue agave. Tequila is such serious business that the Mexican government requires all tequila producers to adhere to strict guidelines known as "Normas." In order to be called tequila, it must be made from a minimum of 51 percent blue agave. Furthermore, the Mexican government officially recognizes four types of tequila.

Tequila in milder, fermented forms was made by the Aztecs for centuries. When the Spanish showed up, they combined their knowledge of distillation with this local favorite and came up with tequila. In the mid 1700s, the king of Spain granted a parcel of land to José Antonio de Cuervo to grow blue agaves. By 1795, José María Guadalupe de Cuervo was granted a concession to commercially produce tequila and "Tequila Cuervo" was born. And from that day to this, they have been the world's leading producer of tequilas.

So, whether you choose an añejo with its deep, aromatic, cognac-like flavor, or a reposado with its rich, full-bodied agave flavor, the next time you're having a tequila, slow down and sip it with a little Sangrita. Enjoy tequila the way they do down south in Mexico, and leave the power-drinking to the gringos.

1. BLANCO

Blanco is basic, inexpensive white tequila used for margaritas and bar mix. It is made from 51% or more blue agave.

2. ORO

Oro, or gold tequila, is either tequila that has a flavor added or an aged tequila that has had a little white tequila added to it. It's commonly used in the United States for premium drinks. It is also made from 51% or more blue agave.

3. REPOSADO

Reposado, meaning rested, is tequila that has been aged in large oak tanks for two to twelve months. This tequila is the most popular among tequila drinkers in Mexico due to the fact that it has a full agave flavor. It is usually made from 100% blue agave. This is also my personal favorite, so before buying I always look for "Reposado" and "100% Agave Azul" on the label.

4. AÑEJO

Añejo is aged for a minimum of one year in small oak barrels. It is considered by many Americans to be the finest of tequilas, mostly because the select-oak aging process creates a flavor reminiscent of premium whisky or cognac, a flavor they recognize. After awhile, most premium tequila drinkers develop a palate for the distinct agave flavor and switch to Reposado.

BANDERA MEXICANA

MEXICAN FLAG

Forget the Margaritas—this is the way to drink tequila. Using the colors of the Mexican flag, you start with a sip of the sangrita (red), follow it with a sip of the tequila (white), and then finish with a sip of the lime juice (green).

1 shot Reposado tequila
1 shot Sangrita Mexicana (recipe page 137)
1 shot key lime juice (or one part lime juice
and one part Squirt Grapefruit Soda)

Serve in three separate, baby brandy snifters. Sip a little, talk a little, smile a little. Ahhh... Mexico.

SERVES 1

SANGRITA MEXICANA

MEXICAN PUNCH

Because this drink is so popular in Mexico, there are many different recipes. I put this one together by talking to several different bartenders in Guadalajara over a four-day visit. Sure, I got a headache, but that's just me, working hard for you!

SANGRITA

1½ cups tomato juice

½ cup clamato juice (very popular in Mexico)

¾ cup orange juice

Juice of 4 key limes

2 teaspoons grenadine

1 teaspoon salt

½ teaspoon black pepper

Dash Worcestershire sauce

Dash A-1 steak sauce (yes, A-1—they love the stuff)

Dash Tabasco

Premium quality Reposado tequila

16 key lime wedges

Stir together all Sangrita ingredients. You will need two 3-inch tall brandy snifters per serving. Fill one half full of Sangrita and the other half full of tequila (about 1 shot in each) and top each with a wedge of lime. Sip a little tequila, sip a little Sangrita, and now and then, take a little bite of the lime wedge. Oh, and one more thing, slow down a little—Life is good.

SERVES 6 TO 8

MARGARITA CONGELADO

FROZEN MARGARITA

Sitting out by the pool with a few friends on a hot day, this frozen treat seems to chase away the heat.

3 shots your favorite tequila

3 shots Cointreau liqueur

Juice of 5 key limes plus 2 whole key limes

3 cups ice

Margarita salt

Toss the tequila, Cointreau, lime juice, and ice in a blender and purée. Pour 2 tablespoons salt on a plate. Cut the limes in half, rim the margarita glasses with lime juice, and turn the glasses upside down, twisting through the salt to coat the rim of the glass. Pour the frozen margarita into the glasses and serve immediately.

MAKES 6 DRINKS

MARGARITA CLASSICO

CLASSIC MARGARITA

This is probably the most well-known drink from Mexico, but if truth be told—and I hate to say this—the classic margarita is more of a tourist drink.

1½ shots your favorite tequila

1½ shots Cointreau liqueur

½ shot key lime juice

Shake with ice and serve.

MAKES 1 COCKTAIL

SANGRE DE MARIA

MEXICAN BLOODY MARY

On a warm, lazy Sunday morning out by the pool, a Mexican Bloody Mary is just the thing to get the day started. Vodka is for Russians!

1½ ounces white tequila

4 ounces tomato juice

2 teaspoons Worcestershire sauce

Juice of 1 key lime

½ serrano chile, seeds removed and finely minced

1 teaspoon prepared horseradish

Sprinkle of freshly ground black pepper

Scallion or lime wedge for garnish

Stir together tequila, tomato juice, Worcestershire sauce, lime juice, serrano chile, and horseradish. Pour into a glass filled with ice, sprinkle with pepper, and garnish.

MAKES 1 COCKTAIL

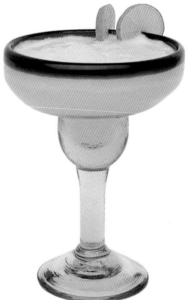

PIÑA FINA

FINE PINEAPPLE

This is the perfect blend of Tequila and pineapple, walking hand-in-hand on a tropical Mexican beach.

1½ cups pineapple, chopped

5 ounces Reposado tequila

Juice of 4 key limes

⅓ cup simple syrup*

Zest of 1 key lime

2 cups of ice

Toss it all in the blender and purée into a slushy frozen treat. Serve in margarita glasses.

SERVES 4

*Simple syrup is equal parts of sugar and water simmered until the sugar is fully dissolved.

GLOSSARY

COMMONLY USED MEXICAN COOKING TERMS

A

Abulón: Abalone
Aceitunas: Olives
Achiote paste: Anneto Seed Paste
Adobe: Sundried, earthen bricks
Agua: Water
Aguacate: Avocado
Aguardiente: Clear, hard liquor made of distilled sugar cane juice
Ajo: Garlic
Albóndigas: Meatballs
Almejas: Clams
Amigos: Friends
Apio: Celery
Arroz: Rice
Atún: Tuna
Avena: Oatmeal
Azúcar: Sugar

B

Barbacoa: An oven-roasted meat, chicken, or fish dish
Bebidas: Drinks
Betabeles: Beets
Bolillos: French-style Rolls

C

Cabra: Goat
Cabrilla: Sea Bass
Cabrito: Little Goat
Cacahuates: Peanuts
Café: Coffee
Calabazas: Pumpkins or Squash
Calamar: Squid
Caldo: Broth
Callos: Scallops or Tripe
Camarones: Shrimp

Camotes: Sweet Potatoes
Canela: Cinnamon
Cangrejo or Jaiba: Crab
Carbón: Charcoal
Carne: Meat
Carne de Res: Beef
Carnitas: Little or Bite-sized Meats
Cazuela: Mexican earthenware pan or pot
Cebolla: Onion
Cebolleta: Green Onion
Cerveza: Beer
Champiñones: Mushrooms
Chicharos: Peas
Cilantro: Fresh leaves and stems of the Coriander Plant
Cocina: Kitchen
Cocinero or cocinera: Cook
Coco: Coconut
Comal: A round griddle used for heating tortillas or toasting foods
Comida: Food
Comino: Cumin
Condimentos: Seasonings
Cordero: Lamb
Crema: Cream

D

Dia de los Muertos: Day of the Dead
Dulces: Sweets
Duraznos: Peaches
Duro: Hard

E

Ejotes: Green Beans
Elote: Corn on the Cob

Ensalada: Salad
Epazote: An Herb similar to Cilantro
Escabeche: Pickled
Especias: Spices

F

Fideos: Noodles
Fiesta: Party, celebration
Flan: Custard
Flauta: Flute
Fresas: Strawberries
Frijoles: Beans
Frutas: Fruits

G

Galletas: Cookies
Ginebra: Gin
Guayaba: Guava

H

Helado: Ice Cream
Higado: Liver
Higo: Fig
Horno: Oven
Huachinango: Red Snapper
Huevos: Eggs

I

Ibarra: a kind of Chocolate

J

Jamón: Ham
Jugo: Juice
Jugo de Naranja: Orange Juice
Jurel: Yellowtail Tuna

L

Langosta: Lobster
Leche: Milk
Lechuga: Lettuce
Legumbres or Verduras:
    Vegetables
Lengua: Tongue
Lenguado: Flounder or Sole
Limón: Lime or Lemon. Lime is
    also known as limócito or
    limón verde.

M

Maiz: Corn off the Cob
Mantequilla: Butter
Manzana: Apple
Mariscos: Shellfish
Masa: Ground Corn Dough
Masa harina: Dough Flour
    (treated cornmeal)
Mayonesa: Mayonnaise
Melón: Melon
Menudo: Tripe & Oregano Soup
Mercado: Market
Miel: Honey
Milpa: Cornfield
Molcajete: A mortar and pestle
    made with volcanic stone
Mole: Mixture
Mostaza: Mustard

N

Naranja: Orange
Nopales: "Young" pads of the
    Prickly-Pear Cactus
Nueces: Nuts
Nuez de Castilla: Walnuts

O

Ostiones: Oysters

P

Paisano: Countryman
Paleta: Sweet, flavored ice on a
    stick (popsicle)
Pan: Bread
Pan Dulce: Sweet Bread
Papas: Potatoes
Parejil: Parsley
Pargo: Snapper
Parilla: Grill
Pastel: Cake
Pato: Duck
Pavo: Turkey
Pay: Pie
Pepino: Cucumber
Pepitas: Hulled Pumpkin Seeds
Pescado: Fish
Pez Espada: Swordfish
Piloncillo: Pilon-shaped raw
    Mexican sugar
Pimienta: Pepper
Piña: Pineapple
Plátano: Banana
Pollo: Chicken
Postres: Desserts
Pueblo: Village
Puerco: Pork

Q

Queso: Cheese

R

Rábano: Radish
Refrescos: Soft Drinks

Relleno: Stuffed
Repollo: Cabbage
Ron: Rum

S

Sal: Salt
Salchicha: Sausage
Sandia: Watermelon
Sopa: Soup

T

Té Caliente: Hot Tea
Té Helado: Iced Tea
Ternera: Veal
Tiburón: Shark
Tocino: Bacon
Tomate: Tomato
Tomatillo: A small, husk-covered
    green tomato
Toronja: Grapefruit

U

Uvas: Grapes

V

Vainilla: Vanilla
Verduras or Legumbres:
    Vegetables
Vino Blanco: White Wine
Vino de Champaña: Champagne
Vino Rosado: Rosé Wine
Vino Tinto: Red Wine

Z

Zanahoria: Carrot

Mad Coyote Joe's love for Mexican food began as a child growing up in Arizona and developed while working in several Scottsdale and Phoenix restaurants. However, he really started his education in Mexican cooking in 1987 as the owner of the Mad Coyote Spice Company, for which he developed fifty-four different spice products. Joe continued learning about Mexican cuisine while working with Hands Across the Border, a cultural exchange program, where he stayed in the private homes of farmers in northern Mexico. This experience was a natural transition into his current job as the host of the extremely popular Southwestern TV show *The Sonoran Grill*.

In the mid-1990s, Joe served as host for the Mad Coyote Joe Annual Charity Cook-Off and Auction. Sponsored by the Chili Appreciation Society of America, it was the largest non-profit chili cook-off in Arizona history. For the past seven years, Joe has also served as head judge and master of ceremonies for the Xerox Southwest Salsa Challenge, which benefits the Hemophilia Association of Arizona. He is an honorary lifetime member of the International Chili Society, and has won numerous awards for his spice mixes and chili. Joe also contributes to *Chili Pepper Magazine* and *Fiery Foods Magazine*.

In addition to his love of Southwestern cuisine, Joe is also an avid guitar player who supports acoustic music in Arizona by performing, volunteering as a guitar teacher, and hosting open-mike shows in his home town of Cave Creek, Arizona, where he lives with his wife, Kathy, and two children, Katie and Joey.